# Just Make Me A Sammich

*Absurd observations*
*from a wild mind*

*by*
### Don Ake

# Contents

# Introduction

I WAS DOWNSIZED FROM MY JOB OF 16 YEARS IN JUNE OF 2009. This was at the very depths of the Great Recession. July 2009 was when the job market was at its worst. Job-hunting "experts" recommended unemployed people write blogs to help them find jobs.

So, I started writing an economic blog "Model T Stock Trends" in September 2009. This was the first time I had written on a regular basis since writing a humor column in college. Surprisingly, the blog was popular and soon acquired an audience of faithful readers. One day on a whim, I injected some humor into a blog post. I was worried that combining humor and economics would be considered unprofessional.

The next day, I saw my friend Alexis and she said, "Enjoyed reading yesterday's post and I really liked the funny stuff!"

I was perplexed. "Really?," I asked.

"Yes, it was the best part," she said.

Humor then became a key element of the economic blog. This is significant because it enabled me to write humor again. And I do mean again because my history writing humor is long. I wrote down some jokes and passed them around the playground when I was 11 years old. I wrote a humor column for my high school paper. I wrote an extremely popular humor column in college. I wrote humorous skits for my church drama team. I even wrote my own material for my stint as a stand-up comedian from 1999 to 2001.

In spite of all this, I did not pursue a writing career after college. I correctly perceived that writers did not make much money for the hard work they do. Instead, I went off into a career in marketing. However, humor writing is what I love, and although I do have various other skills, it's what I do best.

I found a job in April of 2010. I planned to stop writing the economic blog at that time, but my readers wouldn't let me. Then I started considering writing a separate humor blog. I knew this would be fun, but I had absolutely no time to do this. I was working two jobs, teaching part-time at a local university in addition to my day job, and I was writing the economics blog. I had no spare time; I was already overloaded. I kept coming up with ideas for humorous essays, and I almost launched the new blog at two different times but then thought better of it.

However, in May of 2011 I came up with an idea involving Justin Bieber that was too good to pass up, and "Ake's Pains" was born. "Ake's Pains" was the name of my newspaper column at The University of Akron, so it was a rebirth so to speak. I started writing it every other week and sending the link to people on my economic blog mailing list. It was an immediate hit.

There is no theme or concept to the blog. It is whatever I find amusing and want to write about. It is random, satirical, politically incorrect, irreverent and sometimes naughty. It is not profane, too deep, mean or demeaning. The blog has gained a substantial following of a very diverse group of people. People of all races, sexes, incomes, political persuasions and religious affiliations enjoy it. I don't know how I manage to write a humorous, politically incorrect blog that is enjoyed by this wide assortment of individuals. I just do it. Of course, a certain post may offend some people. That is understandable. But if you don't like a certain one, that's okay. The next one will be better.

I write the blog to give people comic relief in a very negative, stressful world. I write it for the person who has had a horrible day at work, comes home, begins reading the blog and starts to literally laugh out loud. As I write this, I put one of my post links on my friend's Facebook page in response to something she had posted. She responded back "(SNORT!) I love you, Don! Glad I read this first thing this morning, cuz no matter what... I'm grinning!!!! Thank you!"

That's the essence; I can't say it any better than that.

So this is my book, a collection of humorous essays from my blog, organized into chapters by subject. It has no theme because the blog has no theme. That can be a good thing however. If you read a piece you don't care for, that's okay. As I said earlier, the next one will be better.

Thank you for purchasing this book. That is your gift to me. And what is contained in the following pages is my gift to you. Read, laugh heartily and enjoy.

You can read the Ake's Pains blog at: http://akespains.blogspot.com

My website is: http://donake.net

Follow on twitter @theakeman

# CHAPTER 1

# Men and Women
# (or Women and Men)

Writing about the relationships between men and women can be difficult. I try to give a fresh, unique outlook on the subject. Of course these essays are inherently sexist – because they are written by a middle-aged man from a guy's perspective. Yet, they are highly respectful of women, because that's who I am. Ask any woman who's ever worked with me or any of my former female students, and they will tell you that I treated them professionally without bias.

Guys like these essays because they know it's the truth. Women enjoy them, sometimes just tolerate them, because they are honest. Mature women have learned men are far from perfect, but they do value honesty. Women in their 20s, who still have a very idealistic view of relationships, don't like my stuff. And that's fine.

## Science Says: Make Me A Sammich

*Preview: This is a running joke that appears many times throughout my posts. So much so that I decided to finally write a separate post about it and include it in the title of the book.*

Every day, all across this great land, men make a familiar demand: "Hey woman, make me a sammich!"

And most often their woman replies: "Get off your a$$ and make your own damn sandwich!"

This dialogue keeps repeating itself in an endless, futile loop in which neither the man nor the woman achieves any degree of satisfaction. So there must be more going on here than appears. If guys were more polite, they might actually get the sammich, and even when they fail, they would irritate women less, which would increase their chances of getting some sex later that day.

But no, the men keep demanding and women keep refusing. I believe this has to do with men desperately trying  to assert their authority in one of the last bastions available to them. In days of yore, men held dominant authority over women. Men were free to do whatever they wanted. They were free to make stupid decisions without interference or guidance. But now women have become educated, informed and empowered (I wanted to use the word "uppity" instead of empowered, but my friend Lori said I couldn't) which has limited the amount of stupid mistakes, and of course fun, that men can make.

At one time, if a woman disobeyed her husband, he would put her across his knee and give her a good spanking.

Those days are long gone, unless of course she is a fan of Fifty Shades of Grey. But then you have to be prepared to aaaah haaaa, and oh boy, and then, oooh weee! But I digress.

Now you may think men are more engaged in this sammich-making issue than women, but you would be mistaken. This subject is very important to women as these examples illustrate:

Many years ago, I was eating my lunch in the company break room when a female acquaintance asked a seemingly harmless question: "Did your wife make that sandwich?" To which I answered: "Yes"

Then this chickee babe went off on a feminista rant (in front of my friends) about what a pig I was forcing my wife to make me sandwiches!

I didn't argue with her because she was so off base. At that time my wife had left the workforce to raise our daughters. She made the sandwiches as a way to support me as the sole moneymaker. I never asked her to make me sandwiches; she did it because she wanted to.

A few years later, another female associate, in the same lunchroom, asked me the same exact question. I was taken back again by the inquiry, but I was relieved to now be able to give the correct answer. "No," I said confidently.

But then Holly Homemaker went off on my spouse, criticizing her for being a dreadful wife and not taking care of my needs. Of course Holly was just as off base as the feminista. Now my children were older and my wife had returned to full-time work. She was extremely busy with everything, so making my sandwiches was my responsibility. I felt absolutely no resentment about this.

I don't understand why these women were so interested in my sandwiches. I felt their questions were intrusive because what happens between the sheets, in this case the sheets of bread, should be private and not the topic of a public, especially workplace, discussion.

So you see this sandwich making stuff is way more important than you realized. This conflict could have raged on unabated, but last year something wonderful, almost miraculous, happened. Scientists conducted a scientific study, using science principles to determine the impact of hunger on married couples. The results of the three-year, extremely scientific project, was reported by the National Academy of, get this, Sciences. The study was even conducted at The Ohio State University, where apparently when they aren't preparing to win football games, actually do scientific stuff like this.

Now, I consider most studies of this type stupid, wasteful, inane, worthless and hogwash, especially those done at Ohio State. Why? Because it diverts resources from important projects like winning even more football games. But the results of this study are so accurate, so important, and so impactful, that I must rate it as the greatest scientific study ever conducted.

The study found that when people are hungry, they are more likely to get angry with their spouses. This combination of hungry and angry, which they labeled "hangry", causes couples to argue and have intense confrontations.

Of course there is a very simple way to cure a man who is hangry and restore marital bliss: WOMEN, MAKE HIM A SAMMICH! Yes, now there is scientific evidence that when men demand a sammich, it is best for everyone if women comply. It has now been scientifically proven by science, so you can't argue against it.

Think of it this way ladies, when your man requests a sandwich, he is not really just asking for something to eat. No, he realizes he is hangry and needs nourishment in order to create a loving, caring, wonderful, soul-mateful relationship with you. One in which he loves and adores you, he asks about your needs and concerns, he truly listens to your every word, and he knows and respects your feelings. That's what he really wants. And you can have all of that just by making a simple sandwich.

And it stands to reason that after the man has eaten the sandwich, he will engage in deep, intimate, meaningful, interaction with the woman, which will lead to something fantastic. The man has intense feelings for the woman because she has relieved his hanger; the woman has strong vibes for the man because he is now showing her love. Their eyes meet, their hearts melt, their souls merge, which leads to: hubba hubba, homina, homina, boing, boing, boing, sis boom bah, ahhhhhhhh!

I would label this "hot sandwich sex" except the term "sandwich sex" is already in use for describing several different activities, which I will not define here. Let's just say the request, "Women make me a sandwich", is totally different than what we are talking about.

No, let's just call it Post-Hangry Unification Coupling. Yes, that's a great name for it.

So women remember this: Next time your husband requests a sandwich, even if he does it in an impolite manner (he's hangry for Pete's sake), science says you should make him the sandwich.

That's right, just make him the damn sammich woman! Make him the damn sammich!

*Postview: The stories about the coworkers are true with absolutely no enhancement needed. You tend to remember when you are publicly called a sexist pig in front of your friends. The study is also 100% legitimate too. Google it if you wish. My interpretation of the findings can be argued, but I would advise against it because you would lose.*

## She's Always A Woman To Me

*Preview: It's always interesting when you tell a young guy the absolute truth and he stares at you like you are crazy. It's called wisdom and you are not born with it. It's only attainable with age. The guys in the office were laughing at Tim's adjustment to married life, so I decided to write this for his benefit. (I used the pseudonym "Tom" in the original post). Plus I just love making fun of stupid scientific studies.*

Often my co-worker Tom will let out a loud sigh, which is followed by one of the following questions. "Why is she doing that?", "Can you believe she made that decision given the choices?", "Why does she have that attitude?", "She is just crazy, right?"

Of course, Tim is a newlywed and in the quest for frequent, hot sex has entered into a very strange, confusing, world. This is a world where a human brain is fueled by estrogen instead of testosterone.

My answer to all his questions is an easy one: "Tim, you married a woman!" He looks at me incredulously and then attempts to explain the situation in great detail and includes his possible explanations of his wife's motives. I listen politely and then render my wisdom gained from many years of marriage and the raising of two daughters.

"You will be very frustrated if you continue to try to figure out the female mind," I caution. "You can't do it. Please stop trying now."

"But she does things that make no sense. Things that are clearly wrong, decisions that I would never make!," Tim protests.

"Unfortunately, these decisions and opinions make perfect sense to her," I explain. Her logic just floats like a butterfly until it lands on the right answer.

"Well that's just stupid!," Tim exclaims.

"Many times she thinks your decisions are narrow-minded and stupid," I say.

"I am never stupid," says Tim. "I am very intelligent and have a college degree!"

"In the words of the prophetess Shania Twain: That don't impress her much," I respond.

"Then what am I supposed to do when she does these idiotic things?," Tim asks.

"First of all, never call her stupid. You respond to it, you react to it, you dance around it, you try to guide it where you want it to go, but never try to understand it," I explain.

Recently, some male researchers in Germany tried to figure out if men could "read" and understand women by using something called "science". They did a study (reported in the journal "*Plos One*") and came to this startling conclusion: MEN CAN'T READ WOMEN'S EMOTIONS. Stop the freakin' presses. This was another worthless study conducted by Captain Obvious. If women scientists were asked to conduct this study, they would have just laughed hysterically. But, Wolfgang and his crew tried to find the secret and failed miserably!

If you need more evidence, mega-genius scientist Stephen Hawking was asked in a 2012 interview if there was anything he could not understand. His reply: "Women, they are a complete mystery to me." So Hawking may be able to understand black holes, but when it comes to understanding other types of, ah, ah, "spaces" (perhaps the spaces between a women's ears), he is ignorant. He is one of the smartest men alive and he is utterly clueless when it comes to understanding women.

One time I asked a gynecologist friend of mine if he understood women. He looked at me dumbfounded and said "of course not". So if a guy who spends all day staring into women's ah, ah, "essence"—yeah essence—can't solve this riddle, then who can?

Well maybe there is one guy who does understand women. Hugh Hefner at 86 years of age married a 26-year old Playboy Playmate in January. His bride is very blonde and very, ah, ah, very healthy. Disregarding any moral judgments or ulterior motives for a moment, you must have some deep, special knowledge to take a bride this bodacious who is 60, yes 60 years younger. (You also need a tremendously strong cardio system and the capability of buying Viagra by the barrel). So it may be possible to understand women, but this knowledge is limited to a privileged few.

So Tim is clueless, but won't admit it. Hawking is a genius, but knows when he is clueless. And Hef knows the secret, doesn't talk about it, but just smiles a lot.

*Postview: Tim wasn't really happy after reading the post. But when the other guys in the office said the stuff was very accurate, Tim conceded that I was probably right. He still doesn't believe much of what I tell him, but he is smart enough to realize that it could be true. That puts him ahead of most guys.*

## Bossy Women and Clueless Men

*Preview: Okay, so I dislike certain "social campaigns" that try to change behavior by slogans or "banning words". I thought the "Ban Bossy" (the word, not the behavior) campaign was extraordinarily stupid, so I had some fun with it. Note that the post ended up making fun of men, way more than disparaging women, because that's how I roll!*

I was delighted when a group of prominent women started a new campaign called "Ban Bossy". We all know how bossy women can be and if they want to ban this behavior, this is something all men can support.

And it is wonderful that Beyoncé is one of the women leading the campaign. Because for me, Beyoncé can be as bossy as she wants. If you were married to Beyoncé, you would cut her lots of slack because she makes about a gazillion dollars and she has luscious thighs like, um, thighs like well, Beyoncé.

Now it could be troubling that Beyoncé might be too busy to make you a sammich, but don't worry. She has so much money that you could have your maid make you a sammich. And not some fat, ugly, maid either. No, you could get one of those leggy French maids with a cute accent. And when Beyoncé is on tour, the maid may even be able to fulfill other domestic type functions as well. But I digress.

Now I believe if women are willing to address this female issue that we men should respond with an improvement campaign of our own. Therefore, I am proposing the "Cut Out Cluelessness" campaign for us guys. I believe cluelessness harms our relationships and if we are able to get more clues, we will understand the feelings of our partners better, and of course most importantly, get more sex.

 Now I know many guys right now are saying: "But Don, I'm not clueless!" And thus you demonstrate the dire extent of the problem. If you think you're not clueless, it means you don't even have a clue about how utter clueless you are. I know you might be very confused right now, but please keep reading because remember, the ultimate goal is to get more sex.

So here is my three-step plan to Cut Out Cluelessness. Now ladies, I know that it will take much more than three steps to accomplish this, but there is only so much wisdom that the male brain can process at one time.

## Step One: Consider the possibility that you could be "wrong"

I know this is a strange concept and the possibility is very small. However, there is still some slight chance that you are not "totally" correct. And if you are in fact "in error", consider that this misjudgment may have caused unforeseen negative consequences that could have upset your partner.

I know you did not intend for these stupid consequences to occur, so it is not really your fault. You do not have to admit you are wrong. However, the possibility exists that you could be. So, do not adamantly claim that you are right. By claiming you are right, you are now clearly doing something wrong, and thus, you will be penalized even if you were originally right. The best thing to do at this point is to shake your head and look bewildered at this mess that just somehow occurred.

## Step Two: Consider the possibility that her explanation (or argument) is indeed rational

This again will be very difficult. While a man's logic is very simplistic, running directly from Point A to Point B, a woman's thought pattern flutters gently like a butterfly, weaving an artistic dance in many directions until it hits you like a missile right between the eyes. Don't try to understand the logic, or you will go stark raving mad. Instead realize that no matter how bizarre the logic, it is rational to her.

I know this will take great effort, but actually try to listen to what she is saying, actually try to understand where she might be coming from. And do not dismiss it as being influenced by her monthly cycle. This is the herculean effort it will take to get you from clueless, to just dense.

## Step Three: Never ask the question "Was it wrong to do that?"

Just the fact that you want to ask this question indicates that the answer is obviously "Yes". But, by actually saying it out loud, you reveal your utter cluelessness. And in response, your mate will not only tell you that this was wrong, but she will rehash a long list of your stupid actions from years gone by. By the end of this rant, she will not just be upset about your most recent faux pas, but the entire historical record. It will send her into Bitchilla mode. Better to not ask the question, but once again drop and shake your head and say, "I guess I should not have done that."

Wait a minute! I just found out that the "Ban Bossy" campaign is not about stopping women from being bossy, but it is about banning the word "bossy" when a woman is actually acting bossy. I don't want any of these bossy, bossy, bossy women to get upset about me calling them bossy so, um, never mind.

*Postview: No bossy women took exception to this one and no clueless guys either. I'm glad everyone took it in fun and I got to fantasize about being married to Beyoncé!*

## Don't Fall For Pushy Women

*Preview: I do take ideas right out of the news when I find a funny angle. With the Internet, I could probably write a post every day if I had the time. This one is from a bizarre news story in 2013.*

Last July, a woman in Montana shoved her newlywed husband off a cliff to his death. This news surprised and shocked almost everyone. Some people (mostly women) were sad for the woman because after finding her soul mate, this "lifetime" commitment was over in a matter of days. Other people (mostly men) wondered how the guy could have made such a poor choice. Now many guys are married to "pushy" women, but this one was a bit "overly pushy".

However, there is one group of guys that was not surprised at all by this news item. These are men who are married to a woman that experiences (notice I didn't say suffers because that would be sexist) Enhanced PMS, or EPMS. I don't think this is a medical term, but it should be. While many people make jokes about PMS, EPMS is not a laughing matter. EPMS can result in you being pushed off a high cliff to your death. EPMS is similar to demonic possession, but unfortunately a Catholic priest is no match for it. You just have to wait for nature to literally run its course.

My guess is that the pushy bride was experiencing EPMS when this unfortunate incident occurred. Of course, EPMS alone did not cause this tragedy. There has to be a "trigger". And of course by a trigger, I am referring to the poor husband's mouth. He obviously said something that he no doubt regretted all the way down until he hit the ground.

Evolution has caused men in close relationships with women experiencing EPMS to adapt to survive. These men don't say anything once the EPMS period (literally, again) starts. Unless of course he is supposed to say something, and then he chooses his words very carefully. Sort of like your life depends on it, because of course, it does. So you have to wonder what this poor guy's last words were. Here are some possibilities:

- Wow, your butt really looks huge in those jeans. Next time we fly, we may have to buy you an extra seat!

- That sammich you made me today was horrible. The bread was stale and it had too much catsup. It was just awful. One of the worst I've ever had. Next time

I tell you to make me a sammich, I expect you to do much better.

- Hey, your sister is looking so smoking hot since she lost all that weight. Maybe you should go on a diet.
- You are spending way too much money on shoes and make-up. How am I ever going to afford my boat when you keep wasting money on stupid crap?
- I can't believe how large your friend Becky's breasts are. They are huge! Her husband sure is a lucky guy.
- You really need to remember to put the toilet seat up after you finish. I'm tired of putting the thing up every time I go in there.
- Quit complaining! You are starting to sound just like your mother and you know how big of a bitch she is.
- Can you pick up the clothes I throw on the floor! I almost tripped over them and hurt myself. I need this floor kept clean.
- I know we were supposed to go out for a romantic dinner to celebrate the night we met, but the guys are having a very important fantasy football league meeting tonight at Hooters. So just make yourself a sammich.
- Do you really have to talk so much? I am going to have to buy me some of those noise cancellation headphones.

Now, I don't know how the trial will turn out, but if I were on the jury I would want to know if the woman was under the influence of EPMS. And if so, what her husband said to set her off. And if she was experiencing EPMS and her husband did say something stupid, I'm letting her walk. Well, that is under one condition; she is required to tell any future suitors on their first date exactly how her first husband died. If you're getting a pushy woman, it's better to know that up front.

*Postview: I was hesitant to discuss PMS because it is a worn-out joke. But I got no complaints about this one. I don't like to make fun of people dying, but I couldn't help myself this time.*

## The Smoking Hot Exemption Rule

*Preview: In January of 2013 Brent Musburger made a seemingly mild comment about a player's girlfriend and the next day more people are talking about it more than the actual game! I defended Musburger by introducing the concept of the "Smoking Hot Exemption" rule. Something all guys realize exists, but women only suspect. This post was very popular, receiving the 4th highest number of "Ake's Pains" hits ever.*

You know the BCS title football game was super boring when the big story the next day was about the comments that announcer Brent Musburger made about Katherine Webb (girlfriend of the Alabama quarterback). Brent had the audacity to refer to Webb as a lovely lady and good looking and even implied that other guys might want a girlfriend that looked like her. Oh the humanity! Oh the blatant heterosexuality!

He didn't say what most guys were thinking at the time: "There is one hot piece of a$$." And he didn't sing "Don't you wish your girlfriend was hot like her?" But even if he had, his behavior would have still been acceptable due to the

"Smoking Hot Exception". The "Smoking Hot Exception" rule, or SHE, states that bad behavior by men is partially or totally excused if there is a smoking-hot female involved. Men instinctively rate women on a scale similar to how chicken wings are listed on a menu; ugly women being equal to "mild" and smoking hot woman equal to "atomic. When men behave badly and there is a woman involved, other men will give him a break depending on where the woman rates on the chart.

It works like this: one guy will be explaining his questionable behavior, another guy will then ask "was she hot?" The first guy will say "she was smoking hot" and then both guys will share a hopeless expression with their hands up it the air. The thought expressed either implicitly or explicitly is "What could I do? She was so smoking hot."

For example:

Guy One: You got another terrible haircut. Why don't you go somewhere else?

Guy Two: The stylist is smoking hot.

Guy One: (with hands up in the air) Oh well, what can you do?

The SHE rule is even used in business:

Executive One: Our VP Sam was caught banging Becky in the storage room. What should we do?

Executive Two: Well, Becky is smoking hot! (both guys with hopeless looks, hands raised up)

Executive One: Oh well, we will just fire Becky and then let's promote Sam because what can we do? She is so smoking hot.

So many "man stories" include the explanation: The saleswoman (the waitress, the stewardess, the stripper, etc.) was so smoking hot that I ended up doing (fill in the blank), but what could I do ........? I am not saying the SHE rule is good or even right, but this is how the world works and you can't really change it much.

Some people have accused Musburger of ogling and leering at Katherine. Now this is of course total bull since he was looking at a video monitor and not at her. Many guys don't even understand what leering is even though it is prohibited by most company sexual harassment policies. As a public service, I will attempt to clarify this in terms guys can understand. Leering is staring intently at a beautiful woman so long that you get caught doing it.

Therefore, leering is a function of the length of the stare. Staring for one second is not leering. Staring for three seconds is not leering. Staring for five seconds is a violation.

So guys, think of it as a five-second count in basketball. You must break eye contact or you can get whistled for a penalty.

The critics say it was creepy for the older Musberger to look at and admire such a young woman. Well, I say it's more creepy that you have any problem with that at all. Brent is a healthy, heterosexual male that naturally reacted to the (smoking-hot) stimulus that was presented to him. Many women do not understand this reaction or the legitimacy of the SHE rule because they do not understand male hormones. Hell, I've had these male hormones since puberty – and I don't understand them. I just try to control them the best I can.

So to all Brent's critics, I wish you would all shut your pie holes and move on to something else equally irrelevant to complain about. And if anyone is offended by this blog post, what could I do? I mean Katherine is just so smoking hot.

*Postview: Okay, I admit this is one of the most sexist things I have written. However, I am not saying this is good, I'm just saying this is how things are. And of course, this does not ever condone harassment or breaking the law. The part about the woman getting fired from her job and the guy getting promoted was actually based on a real incident. I was not the guy involved however!*

# CHAPTER 2

# Celebrity Absurdities

Our society is outrageously obsessed with celebrities. Of course, the presence of the Internet makes it so much worse. Every day, you can read about all sorts of ridiculous things regarding celebrities. So when these people do or say something stupid, I write about it. And of course, there is a post here about me trying to become like a certain celebrity. It's not like I'm obsessed with the guy or anything because I'm not, really, I'm not.

## Gazing Upon the Royal Jewels

*Preview: In 2012, a band of paparazzi was stalking Kate Middleton, the Duchess of Cambridge trying to get photos of her, well, naughty bits. It was like something you would try to do back in junior high school only these were professional photographers and they could get big bucks for getting a shot of the trophy. And oddly enough, they were surprisingly successful at delivering the "goods". I took the high road and defended Kate's honor. I hope she appreciated that.*

**19**

Truth #1 – The Internet is a wonderful thing because it allows you to see anything and everything. The Internet is also a terrible thing because it allows you to see anything and everything, including things that you should not see.

Truth #2 – Teenage boys have a burning desire to see things they are not allowed to look at. As men grow older this desire is tempered because men are permitted to see more things than boys. However, this temptation never really goes away.

And now, these two truths are on a collision course so epic that civilization may temporarily come to a grinding halt. The alarming event in question is the soon to be released topless photos of Kate Middleton, the Duchess of Cambridge.

Now this wasn't a case of "Princesses Gone Wild". Kate did not flash her goodies to get some beads. She already has all the "real" beads she needs. No, some photographer, who reportedly is a former teenage boy, snapped some long-range photos of Kate while she was sunbathing topless on a private beach.

This is an outrageous violation of Kate's privacy. They may post the photos, but this is something that should not be seen by anyone. No one should look at it. This means that soon after the photos are posted, millions of men throughout the world will jump on the Internet to get a glimpse of the royal ta-tas. I fully expect the entire Internet to totally freeze up until every man in the world with an Internet connection is able to adequately ogle the duchess. This threatens to crash the entire Internet as we know it.

To save the Internet, we may have to bring in Officer Barbrady from South Park to declare: "Move along people.

Nothing to see here." And I do believe there is not going to be much to see. While Kate is a certified royal babe, she is considered to be "lithe". This means that she could not get a job at Hooters. She has no trouble jumping rope and she can easily see her feet while standing. Her cups, even when measured in milliliters, appear (when clothed) to be modest.

Of course, after the men of the world finish gawking, many women will also view the photos. They will want to see how they measure up compared to the Duchess. All women want to be princesses and a duchess is very close to that. Many will think: "Look at that. My goodies are better than her royal jewels. Perhaps the Duke would like to upgrade from princess size to queen size." They believe this because in life, as in poker, two queens beat a small pair.

This scandal will be very embarrassing for poor Kate. I know it is sure to be very awkward the next time I see her. I will have to be careful not to talk about my vacation to the Flatlands and not to mention the firmness of the mini-muffins being served at the party. And if Kate had any ideas about discretely enhancing the royal treasure chest, she can foggetaboutit because everyone will have seen a "before" photo.

On the other hand, the photos represent just how far we have progressed as a civilization. In olden days, a commoner could be put to death for even accidently viewing royal naughty bits. But now, everyone can see the spectacles from the privacy of their own homes. Heck, you can even project the image on your big screen TV if you wish.

Now some will argue that you should not view these photographs because of their salacious content. But I am giving men everywhere permission to look based on creative grounds. You see, these photos should not be considered pornographic, but because they are of royalty, they should be considered art. They are just as much art as the ancient statues of some old chicks, which displayed large, naked jugs. So guys, go ahead and enjoy an enchanting, inspiring experience. Ahhhhhh, euphoric.

Just don't peruse the photos too long. And remember; keep both hands on the keyboard at all times.

*Postview: Women enjoyed this post more than I expected. Many women want to grow up to be princesses, and I was in a strange way defending Kate's honor. Because it was a very hot topic at the time, it is the second most popular "Ake's Pains" ever.*

## I Am Pitbull, So Don't Stop My Party

*Preview: I have a shaved head, which of course hides all male pattern baldness. All of a sudden, I see this guy Pitbull in beer commercials. He has a shaved head like me, but he is very popular with people, especially the hot, young ladies. I conclude that the only difference between him and me are his cool sunglasses. So of course, I all I need are a pair just like his (sunglasses, that is).*

A couple of my male friends dealt with mid-life crises by buying very expensive, red convertibles. Now I am going through my own mid-life crisis. However, I'm too large to jump in and out of a sports car, and you can forget about the thrill of the wind blowing through my hair. So I have dealt with my situation in a much more rational and mature way: I decided to prove to the world that I've still "got it" by trying to be like the rapper Pitbull.

Pitbull is that cool guy with the shaved head in those beer commercials who apparently is not very concerned about curfews because he keeps shouting "Don't stop the party." He is very popular because when he raps he gets so into it that he gyrates as if he is having a seizure. People love this, but if he ever does have a seizure during a concert, he is toast because everyone will keep partying instead of calling 911. I mean "don't stop the party", right?

Pitbull's other trademark is his super-stylish sunglasses which he wears all the time. Since I already am sporting the shaved head, it was time to visit the yuppie sunglasses store at the mall. I showed the babelicious saleswoman Katie a photo of Pitbull wearing his super cool shades and she found three pairs that were "bull worthy". I found the one I liked the best and looked in the mirror. I was wearing my black leather jacket and the visual effect was stunning.

"I look bad-ass," I exclaimed.

"You do look bad-ass. You look very bad-ass," said Katie.

Of course, when a hot, young, chick tells a guy my age that he looks "bad-ass", you know he really has to have those sunglasses.

There was only one more detail. It is very important that a guy's sunglasses enable him to stare at women's boobs without being detected. It allows you to leer without getting caught by the leerie nor your significant other.

"Can you tell that I am staring at your boobs?," I asked Katie.

Katie looked carefully and said, "I can see your eyes, but I can't tell where they are focused."

She then proceeded to pose from various distances and angles while I admired her body (this really happened).

When I pointed out to Katie that I had just convinced a smoking hot woman to let me stare at her in various positions, she blushed big time. I immediately apologized; worried that I had crossed the line.

That's perfectly fine, Katie cooed. "In fact that sounded like something Pitbull would say. I think those glasses are working for you. You have a much more confident attitude."

At this, I immediately removed the sunglasses because I was afraid that Katie was going to embrace me right there in the store. The total came to $234.75, which is probably more than I have paid for all the sunglasses I have ever owned in my life.

Now some of you might be thinking that this is too much money to pay for a pair of sunglasses when there are so many starving children in Africa. I say the sunglasses are cheap compared to paying $50,000 for a sports car, and of course I am writing a check for $49,765.25 to the Donation Opportunity Now African Kids Enrichment fund. It makes me feel good because it is going to such a worthy cause.

I decided I had to wear the sunglasses all the time (including inside) because I paid so much for them, and of course, because this is what Pitbull does. However, this did cause me some unexpected problems. First of all, I was tripping over everything at work because it was too dark. Then during a big meeting, an executive suddenly barked out, "Ake, take off those sunglasses. What are you doing, daydreaming behind those things?"

Of course, I wasn't daydreaming! What type of lackey does he think I am? I was just staring at the boobs of the woman sitting across the table.

Then one day I was talking to my friend Sally in the grocery store. She was telling me about her weekend plans when she stopped suddenly and questioned, "Are you staring at my boobs?"

A gentleman will never admit this (although I doubt very much if women mind when Pitbull stares at their boobs) so I said: "No, of course not. Why do you ask?"

"Because you are wearing sunglasses and I am wearing a $100 push-up bra! You should be staring at my boobs!," Sally exclaimed.

The other bad thing about wearing sunglasses is that it impairs your peripheral vision, which means I never saw the bitch slap coming. It stung really bad and there was ringing in my ears for a couple days, but most importantly, the sunglasses were not damaged.

After that incident, I am no longer wearing my sunglasses indoors, or at night, for that matter. I can't wait for summer to get here so I can truly transform into Pitbull. I hope people start calling me Mr. Bull. Of course, people often refer to me as Mr. Bull-something already.

*Postview: The narrative at the sunglasses store is very close to the truth. I love people who don't take life too seriously, and Katie was a great sport. I gave her a signed copy of the post afterward. I did not, however, wear my sunglasses to work. I may act stupid – but I'm not that stupid.*

### I Dated Taylor Swift
### (and she wrote a song about it)

*Preview: Hey, everyone else was dating Taylor Swift at the time – so why not me! I got the idea for this post when I asked myself: What would happen if I dated Taylor Swift? And then I was "inspired".*

Recently I had the awesome experience of dating Taylor Swift. Now you might wonder how I attracted the affection of Ms. Swift, but I was wearing my $230 designer Pitbull sunglasses and chicks just can't resist them. I think she may have actually thought I was Pitbull when we began the relationship. In addition, she is originally from Pennsylvania, so maybe I had my Pennsylvania Dutch mojo going.

Unfortunately, the relationship lasted only 15 minutes. No, this wasn't speed dating. Apparently courtships move much faster these days. However, I found out afterward that brief relationships are common for Taylor and that I actually lasted longer than several of her other boyfriends.

Now you might think she left me because the sex was bad, but let me assure you that was not the case. I can say this because the relationship lasted only 15 minutes and my little blue pill takes about an hour to work. The sex wasn't the problem, but maybe it was my Aqua Velva aftershave.

I know I should not be dating young chicks at my age, especially since I am married. But c'mon, this is TAYLOR

SWIFT! I mean she is smoking hot, she is super rich, and she does not appear to be too bright. In other words, many guys would consider her the "perfect woman"!

But it ended much too quickly. Apparently there was a problem with our ages. Okay, so there was a problem with MY age. She said she wanted to go back to December, but just not May/December. She said she was afraid someday I might leave drool drops on her guitar. So the relationship came to an abrupt end.

When I was younger I would have been crushed by this rejection, but now I just got some nachos and everything was fine. I did text her the next day, but she texted back "We are never, ever, ever, getting back together."

I thought that was the end of this incident until I turned on the radio a few weeks later and heard Taylor wailing a song she had written about our fling:

> I really thought you were the one, but I am older
> than your son.
>
> I wanted me some six-pack abs, not 6 big pounds
> of belly flab.
>
> You were so suave and debonair – didn't notice all
> your ear hair.
>
> Now I'm REALLY, REALLY, REALLY MAD! –
> 'cuz you're old enough to be my dad.
>
> da da, - da,da, - dadadada – da da
>
> You said you were European, but all the time,
> you're a peein'.
>
> I just wanted to frolic in Niagara, but you said you
> needed some Viagra.
>
> Yeh, yeh, yeh, when I'm with you, I feeling "52".

Now I'm REALLY, REALLY, REALLY MAD! –
'cuz you're old enough to be my dad.

da da, - da,da, - dadadada – da da

 So as the mega hit "Old Enough To Be My Dad" rockets up the charts, I am totally embarrassed, and Taylor, she makes a few more millions. But I have learned my lesson. I am not going to be used and have my heart broken by a hot, young celebrity ever again. However, if anyone happens to have Shania Twain's cell number, please send it over.

And in response to Ms. Swift's song, I have decided to write a song of my own about the relationship.

Okay this song writing stuff can't be too difficult ....

I should have bought you flowers.

I should have held your hand.

Should have gave you all my hours ...

Wait, what? Bruno who? From where? So Bruno from Mars has already done this? Okay, let's start over.

All you young, wild, girls

You make a mess of me.

All you young, wild girls ...

What now? Are you freaking kidding me? That Bruno guy again!

That's it. Just forget I said anything about any of this.

*Postview: The four Swift song references, if you are not a fan, are: Back to December (not May/December), Teardrops On My Guitar (not drool drops), We Are Never Ever Getting Back Together", (Feeling) 22 (not 52)*

*My comedian friend, Taylor Mason, sent me a note complimenting me on this post. It meant a lot coming from a professional.*

## No Bieber Shots Please!

*Preview: This was the very first "Ake's Pains". I had told myself for about three months that I was absolutely not going to start a humor blog because I had absolutely no time to write it. Then I saw people going crazy over this 17-year old freakazoid and I just knew this was too funny to pass up and "Ake's Pains" was born.*

I just heard about the latest teen pop sensation, Justine Bieber. Apparently, Justine is very, very popular. She is all over the radio, television, magazines, and this new, very popular thing that people are calling the Internet.

Now you may think that Justine is just like the other former teen pop tarts like Britney, Christina, and Joe Montana's daughter, Hannah. These teen stars use suggestive videos and "hooker" outfits to increase their popularity in our sex-obsessed culture. However, the wonderful thing is Justine is not anything like that. She is very plain looking with slim hips and a relatively flat (hopefully still developing) chest. She dresses modestly, wears little jewelry and even appears to wear no make-up. She shows no cleavage because she has no cleavage! Justine does have a very cute, unique, hairstyle that surely will be copied by young women everywhere a la Jennifer Aniston.

It is refreshing in this day and age to see a young woman succeed on talent alone. Justine is serving as a strong role model to teen girls everywhere proving that you don't have to dress or act sexy to be successful in this world. And the girls are responding very positively to Justine by attending her concerts in large numbers and screaming loudly in approval when she enters the stage. Teen girls also account for the great majority of her album and 8-track sales.

We can only hope that Justine remains pure and does not follow the path of those other slutty pop stars. These women kept pushing the limits of sexual expression, which ultimately results in them showing their hoohah. This is sad. There is no reason for this. No one was questioning if they were indeed women, but they all feel the need for some reason to flash the hoohah. These women may have great voices, but there is nothing exceptional about their hoohahs. Sure the all the guys look. Show a guy a hoohah and he will look at it. But you're a singer, not a porn star, so it's better to remember to put on some panties before leaving your crib.

They probably do it for publicity reasons, but often the hoohah ends up overshadowing the star. They announce on the radio, "Here is the latest release by Britney who incidentally showed her hoohah again last week." Also, "In an exclusive interview Christina's hoohah said while it enjoys the exposure and attention, it is not looking forward to January's concert in Toronto."

In response to this obsession with what our pop stars look like and how sexy they are, there is a new television show called "The Voice" where the contestants are judged by their voices alone. This is a good start. I think a better television show would be one called "The Hoohah" where the female singing contestants would show their hoohahs first. Celebrity judges (maybe Hugh Hefner, Charlie Sheen and Ted Nugent) would select the woman with the best hoohah and she would be awarded voice lessons. We would then follow her progression as a singer every week. This would be similar to reverse engineering, if you will. You may scoff at this idea, but you know you would watch the first episode.

But all this is what makes Justine special. Never say never, but I don't think there is any chance that she would ever sell-out and show the world her hoohah. Justine has restored my faith in the youth of America. Let's just hope that other female teen vocalists will follow in her footsteps.

*Postview: I have no idea how many people read this first post because the blog site did not count hits at that time. But, I must have been pleased with my first effort because I kept writing, even though I had absolutely no time to do so.*

## World Peace Threatens the World Peace

*Preview: Basketball player Ron Artest was at the end of his career when he changed his name in a desperate attempt to retain some relevance. His new name is "Metta World Peace". This was laughable because he was one of the most dirty, violent, non-peaceful players in the game! This is the equivalent of Lady Gaga changing her name to Mother Teresa. The post is from April 2012.*

Everything in the world was going fine (okay if you ignore Syria, North Korea, Iran, Afghanistan and several other countries which are too difficult to spell) and then the unthinkable happened.

WORLD PEACE HAS ELBOWED SOMEONE IN THE HEAD!!!!!!!!!

I am not making this up. It is the absolute truth: WORLD PEACE HAS ELBOWED SOMEONE IN THE HEAD!!!!!!!!!

A bit of clarification is in order. Before the pro basketball season began, Ron Artest of the Los Angeles Lakers legally changed his name to "Metta World Peace". He did this either to promote love and harmony on the planet or because he is an attention whore. He was having a very peaceful season until recently, when during a game, he violently elbowed an opposing player in the head giving him a concussion. And therefore:

WORLD PEACE HAS ELBOWED SOMEONE IN THE HEAD!!!!!!!!!

If you are going to carry the name of World Peace, your mission in life becomes to promote world peace everywhere and in everything you do. And that includes when somebody

tries to steal the basketball away from you. If your name is World Peace, you absolutely cannot go around elbowing people in the head.

Because of this shocking incident, I believe there should be qualifications if you change your name to something of significance. In this case, if you want the name "World Peace" you should have to prove you are fully committed to the cause. That's right; I would only give this name to a dope-smoking hippie.

You would be required to have long hair, a headband and a beard. But you would have to bathe at least once a week (difficult to promote World Peace if you smell offensive). And you would have to pass a drug test. Of course this drug test would be unique in that you would have to test positive for marijuana; the higher the content, the better. This would prove you are a genuine hippie and it would also mean you are mellow enough to not elbow someone in the head. And, as you know, this is important because:

WORLD PEACE HAS ELBOWED SOMEONE IN THE HEAD!!!!!!!!!

I think as punishment World Peace should be forced to change his name to: "I Elbowed Someone in the Head". This name would be more fitting and would serve as a deterrent in case you were tempted to elbow someone in the head. This new name would be very cumbersome when filling out forms. It would be awkward when introducing yourself to new people and it would be embarrassing when ordering pizza.

And he should be punished. President Obama has worked very hard to establish world peace, except for in Syria, Iran, Afghanistan and those other unspellable places. Now all this has all been ruined because:

WORLD PEACE HAS ELBOWED SOMEONE IN THE HEAD!!!!!!!!!

What type of example do we set when we have World Peace getting all irritated and going off like a madman and elbowing someone in the head? Do we really expect the tyrants in Darfur to respect us when we have this type of hijinks occurring? Come on America, we are so much better than that!

And now, as a result of this incident, something even worse has happened. The NBA commissioner has suspended

World Peace for seven games, which is about two weeks of time. You read that correctly. Please do not panic, but:
WORLD PEACE HAS BEEN SUSPENDED FOR TWO WEEKS!!!!!!!!!!!!
Now you know all types of hell are going to break loose around the world because of this. We may not even have to wait for the Mayan calendar to expire before the apocalypse hits.

Because WORLD PEACE HAS ELBOWED SOMEONE IN THE HEAD, the following things have happened:
North Korea has threatened to give South Korea a noogie of "unprecedented and peculiar means".
Iran is making plans to poke Israel in the eye.
Even Switzerland is rumored to be considering kicking Austria square between the Alps.
All this needless violence, just because:
WORLD PEACE HAS ELBOWED SOMEONE IN THE HEAD!!!!!!!!!!

*Postview: This post was not that popular, but I still find it very amusing. I don't think most people believed that someone would actually change their name to "Metta World Peace" but you can look it up!*

# CHAPTER 3

# Miscellaneous Stuff

"AKE'S PAINS" IS ABOUT EVERYTHING AND ANYTHING I FIND amusing so it stands to reason there are posts, which don't fit into any specific category. Some of these were prompted by humorous articles in the news; some involved strange things that happened to me outside of home or work; and other subjects are significant (and humorous) to me for whatever reason. Yes they are random. Yes they are funny. Please enjoy.

## I Have Finally Changed My Underwear

*Preview: It takes a secure man to blog about his underwear, especially when he knows women of all ages, around the world, will be reading about it. Because my underwear is obviously important, and very close to me, I wrote an entire post about it.*

We live in a time of great innovations. Over the last decade, we have seen MP3 players, tablets, smart phones and big screen televisions, etc. But in my opinion, the greatest recent creation has been something surprisingly low-tech; it is the boxer brief.

This is one of the greatest inventions of all time. This wonderful undergarment combines the freedom of the boxer, with the security of the brief. Freedom and security—these are the same concepts that make America great. This is truly American underwear, although the last pair I bought was, in fact, made in Indonesia. But regardless, let freedom ring and be secure at the same time!

These concepts are very important to a man and more specifically, to his man parts. Remember the Seinfeld episode involving Kramer getting so frustrated because neither boxers nor briefs satisfied "his boys" that he just gave up and decided to go "commando".

But now there is the grand compromise. The boxer and brief come together into a pair of uber-wear that is extremely pleasing to your man parts and thighs. If our government leaders would compromise like this, our country would be so awesome that we could take over Canada and Mexico without any resistance. After we gave their leaders the finest boxer briefs available, they would be so delighted they would sign over their territories without a fight.

For years there was a lively debate over which was better, the boxer or the brief. President Bill Clinton even commented on the subject in 1994, although we know his focus was never on getting into "men's" undergarments. Once a younger co-worker of mine became discouraged because a survey said women preferred men wearing boxers over briefs. My friend was a brief wearer and said to me, "Don, I just don't get it. Why would women say that?"

I told him that he is never going to understand women. But I also told him that it doesn't matter which they prefer because once you get to the point where a woman can see your skivvies, all that matters is that they [your skivvies] are clean and atheistic (without any hole-liness). You are just going to pull them off quickly anyhow, so you don't need to make a change over to boxers.

But this once heated debate is now totally over. The boxer brief is truly superior to any other underwear. The only reason boxers and briefs are still sold is that men have issues with changing their underwear. Men put as much apprehension into making a decision to change their type of underwear as they put into changing their religion. Under no circumstance do you want to upset your man parts.

I can still remember purchasing my first pair of boxer briefs. I nervously looked around to see if anyone was watching me at the underwear rack. I made my selection and kept it hidden under my arm while waiting in line. I was worried the cashier might give me a strange look for buying such "weird" shorts. She didn't flinch, but she did have to swipe my credit card for me since I was shaking so badly.

But when I got home and put on the new boxer briefs for the first time, it was like having a religious experience. If my man parts could, they would have been singing for joy. I have been sporting boxer briefs ever since.

I believe the inventor of the boxer brief should win the Nobel Peace Prize because this invention has enabled my man parts and thighs to live in perfect peace. The war in my pants has ended. We have har-mony, we have tranquility, and we are all living in one accord (with no chafing!).

And it's getting even better! My newest pairs of boxer briefs are treated with an anti-microbial to inhibit odor. When I am wearing these, I feel like I can meet any challenge, scale any mountain and vanquish any foe. If they ever invent a pair of boxer briefs with a muffler on the back, I will rule the world!

*Postview: This post was actually very popular among women. I think they find it highly amusing that men now have difficult choices regarding undergarments. I think guys may have read this blog more for educational purposes because men do not discuss matters such as this with other guys, without breaking the "man code".*

## Bad Pizza Man, Really Bad Pizza

*Preview: Why does this stuff happen to me? I don't know, but people sure like reading about my weird escapades. By the way, the term "Bad Pizza" comes from my former co-worker Mark who used the term frequently to describe anything and everything that went wrong with anybody: "That's bad pizza."*

The summer of 2012 has been one of the hottest on record in Northeast Ohio. During most extremely hot summers, there is that one time, that one day, when you are so hot or uncomfortable that it burns (a very appropriate term here) into your long-term memory.

This is my "hottest" memory of the scorching summer of 2012. It was a Friday and the temperature had reached 98 degrees. I called my favorite pizza place after work as I often do on a Friday, and ordered two, two-topping pizzas. I was told the order would be ready in 30 minutes which is longer than their standard 20 minute wait, so I knew that they were busier than normal. What I didn't know is that because of the 98-degree heat, everyone and their brother decided not to cook dinner but was instead ordering pizza.

I got to the pizza joint a few minutes early and there was only one customer waiting. So, I decided to stay in my car for a while because I assumed that it would be hot inside. When I finally entered, I had assumed correctly because the temperature in the pizza joint had to be close to 90 degrees (even with air conditioning),and the air was thick with pizza scent. It was so thick; it was difficult to even breathe. And this was because of the massive amount of pizza orders that came in right after mine. Every oven was baking. The employees were scrambling like mad to make and bake the pizzas.

The first person in line got her order. But by now, there were five people in line behind me. The staff had not been able to wait on me because they were still rushing to make all the pizzas. I had already been waiting over five minutes in the Italian sauna. Sweat was running off my shaved head and dripping profusely off my chin. I was very hungry and the thick smell of baking pizzas was strangely appetizing and nauseating at the same time. After waiting 10 minutes I thought I was going to die of pepperoni fume asphyxiation. It was so uncomfortable that I did consider leaving at one point, but I stayed since I still needed something for dinner.

At the 15-minute mark, the guy asked who had "two large". I gave him my name, he checked the bill and I was on my way. You bet the car air conditioner was fully cranked on my drive home.

When my wife opened the first box she exclaimed, "What did you order?"

"The usual," I replied.

"Well this is not it!," she declared.

Now, we are generally not that picky when it comes to pizza toppings. I would guess that 99% of pizza topping combinations would be acceptable to us. Heck, if there were three or more standard toppings on the pizza, I would have even come out ahead. Of course, this is what happens to normal people; it's not what happens to me. (I will never run out of topics for this blog because my life is so wacked out.) The first pizza contained jalapenos. Just jalapenos. Lots of jalapenos. Imagine a pepperoni pizza covered edge to edge in pepperoni, but instead of pepperoni, it is covered

with sliced jalapenos! I do like jalapenos, but my wife does not. But, I had to prove to my wife this wasn't a total disaster. So, I actually tried to eat the super jalapeno pizza. (And remember, this was after almost getting sick in the pizza sauna) I was barely able to get one piece down and part of the second before I gave up. This wasn't just bad pizza, it was nasty pizza. It was the nastiest pizza I have ever eaten in my life. And it made one nasty trip through my body causing issues at every stop. It inflamed my taste buds, it irritated my stomach lining, and it was not too kind to my hemorrhoids upon departure.

The second pizza was a disappointing, unpalatable, plain without cheese pizza. Both pizzas were undercooked because, of course, my pizzas were supposed to come out of the oven before these pizzas from hell. My wife and daughter were able to eat some of the partially cooked dough with to- mato sauce (the second pizza). So we did not starve and I do realize that there are starving people in Africa, but they prob- ably would not have eaten the super jalapeno pizza either.

What type of person orders these types of weird pizzas? Using my Sherlock Holmes detective skills, I deduced it was a Hispanic vegetarian. I am glad that we live in a country where Hispanic vegetarians have the freedom and the opportunity to order super jalapeno pizzas, but why, oh, why, did I have to get his order by mistake?

However as disappointed as I was to receive these pizzas, the Hispanic vegetarian had to be even more displeased to get mine. He could not have been very happy with my sausage-bacon and pepperoni-ground beef pizzas. Ironically, while his pizzas were barely edible for me, my pizzas were probably totally inedible for him. That's bad pizza. Bad pizza for everyone! Bad, bad pizza in the hot summer of 2012.

*Postlude: I kept my receipt and after explaining the super jalapeno screw up, the pizza parlor graciously gave be a credit for two pizzas, which of course I took care to order on a much cooler Friday.*

*Postview: This post caused an unexpected debate at my office. Stan said this post was stupid because you should always check your pizzas before you leave the place to make sure your order is correct. Others said that if you open the box, you let the heat escape and you get home with cold pizza. But Stan's wife is a rather intolerant person (to be polite) and if he came home with a plain pizza, it wouldn't be the only thing missing its sausage. So I guess Stan should check his order every time! To check or not to check, that is the question ....*

## These Butts Are Big And I Cannot Lie

*Preview: When I am reading a news article and I can't stop laughing, I know it is a great blog subject. I just have to restate the facts and then put my own warped perspective on it. And it is so easy to Google subjects to confirm "I am not making this stuff up".*

Ever since the rapper Sir Mix-A-Lot sang "I Like Big Butts and I Cannot Lie" in the song "Baby Got Back", many women have desired to have the delicious derrieres like the ones featured in that music video. Unfortunately, this trend has led to the emergence of black market butt enhancement surgery. (I learned about this alarming practice in a recent newspaper article. Incredibly, I am not making this up!)

Legitimate butt enhancement surgery performed by a doctor costs around $4,500, but the black market variety, usually performed in someone's garage is a "bargain" at $2,100. I don't know which is worse, paying two grand to let a non-doctor perform a medical procedure on you or actually being the person charging money and performing this surgery on others using industrial tools.

The article said women are willing to undergo the black market surgery to look better in bikinis, fill out their jeans and most importantly, to get gigs performing in rap videos. I know this seems ludicrous to many women who desire a smaller rump, not a bigger one. This surgery is desired primarily by younger women because, of course, the size of a woman's posterior can expand to enormous proportions as she ages. It can therefore be very dangerous to accelerate this expansion. Older women want smaller, not bigger butts.

I am not opposed to women having cosmetic surgery if the conditions are right and they have the cash, but I don't think this is the best option for most women. And it is not really necessary for filling out your jeans since there are inserts, rump falsies if you will, that can do that for much less money. Of all the cosmetic surgeries a woman could have, butt enhancement surgery would seem to provide the least bang for the buck. Er, let met rephrase that. On second thought, no, that statement is fine as is. Although I know Sir Mix-A-Lot would disagree and he cannot lie.

The only two positive things you can say about the back-alley butt surgeons are that they are both entrepreneurs and innovators. They did not try to emulate legitimate butt enhancement surgery, which consists of inserting an implant in each cheek. No, they developed their own method. This consists of making an incision, inserting a tube under the skin, and then using an air compressor to pump industrial-grade silicone into each buttock. The incision is then sealed using cotton balls and super glue. (According to the article).

So while a doctor purchases his equipment and supplies from a medical supply firm, the illegal operators buy their stuff at the Home Depot.

Clerk:     Wow, another 55-gallon drum of industrial silicone. Are you a contractor?

Buttman:   Er, yeah. That's it. I'm a contractor.

Clerk:     What type?

Buttman:   Um, let's just say I specialize in improving back doors and back porches.

This silicone injection method actually works – for a while. Over time, the silicone begins to set up and the "patient" literally becomes a hard ass. Unfortunately, the silicone is extremely difficult to remove and complications can result in serious illness and even death. (She wanted an ass to die for and she did).

But apparently some women are willing to take this risk to achieve their goal of being "rump shakers" in the next big music video. It does have to be very traumatic for these women to be auditioning for a video and hearing the director shout: "Stop! Okay, third bitch from the left. Get your bony ass out of here! Put on your skinny jeans and go home!"

And it is very rare to have a rump awesome enough to be in a music video. As research for this post, I streamed "Baby Got Back" to my 60" HD TV, and after viewing it I can honestly say: "I fear big butts and I cannot lie."

However, I do have compassion for these women. So, I have established the charitable organization "Booty For Booties" to raise money so that woman with malnourished asses can receive legitimate butt enhancement surgery performed by a medical doctor.

This will allow these formerly flat-cheeked ladies to pursue their hopes and dreams of being big-butted, music video stars.

*Postview: This post is by far the most popular "Ake's Pains" ever with over 27,000 total hits and huge worldwide readership. What happened after this was posted was so bizarre, I wrote the following blog post about this post.*

*But there was a sinister element to why this post was so popular. To find the reason, see the end of this chapter.*

# Bigger Butts Lead To Better Blogs

*Preview: Wow, if I got so many hits on my first "butt blog", maybe I could recreate the results with another.*

I blogged about a wide variety of subjects in 2013, but by far the most popular post was "These Butts Are Big And I Cannot Lie" which took a humorous look at black market butt enhancement surgery. At first, the readership of this post was about average, but then after about three weeks the post started getting over 200 hits each day.

Of course I thought this was because people had finally discovered my spectacular blogging ability and started sharing and reposting this superb literary work. But then I realized the hits were the result of the post showing up very high on Google searches. It had inadvertently achieved great search engine optimization.

So now when people search for "big butts", "big a$$" big booty, and other similar butt-related topics, they are directed to my blog post. This is odd because the post is not sexually oriented. Sure, there is a photo of a woman in a provocative pose, but she is fully clothed and it is more humorous than indecent.

But according to my blog statistics, many people are looking for big butts on the Internet. And this demand for big butts is worldwide. They love big butts in Germany. And big butts are also surprisingly popular in Saudi Arabia, India and Morocco. My butt blog also has even generated hits from Iran. Iranians like big butts, but they probably lie about it.

Of course I thought about the potential of "big-butt" blogging. I considered starting a blog concentrating on nothing but large derrieres. If big butts are that popular then someone needs to fill this void (I mean figuratively!). Apparently, based on the German popularity: "It's vat da people vawnt!"

But then I realized that exploiting this dalliance for big butts would be wrong. It was at this point I made a vow to never, ever write another blog post on the topic of big butts. And I am determined to keep this vow no matter what. You have my word on this. And this includes not posting any other big butt photos in my blog, like the ones that appear in this post) just for the purpose of generating a massive number of hits.

I thought this commotion about big butts was just about over when I received the following phone call:

| | |
|---|---|
| Caller: | May I speak to Mr. Ake's Pains |
| Me: | I guess that's me |
| Caller: | Well this is Sir Mix-A-Lot. Mr. Pains I hear your recent blog post has revived a worldwide interest in big butts and I was wondering if you would work with me to revive my career. Perhaps you have heard that I like big butts and I cannot lie. |
| Me: | I may have heard that once or twice before, but I can't help you. My blog was not about guys who like big butts. It was on guys who illegally create big butts. And I don't really prefer women with big butts. |

| | |
|---|---|
| Mix-A-Lot: | Really Pains? You other brothers can't deny! |
| Me: | But I have to deny. |
| Mix-A-Lot: | I think that is so wrong. I think you are practicing "big booty discrimination". |
| Me: | For the record, I do not discriminate against women's butts on the basis of size, age, race or national origin. However, I do explicitly believe that the shape of the booty is more important than the size of the booty. |
| Mix-A-Lot: | Come On Akes. Even white boys got to shout "baby got back!" Admit it. You want a motor in the back of your Honda. |
| Me: | I still prefer shape over size. And I'm afraid my Honda riding days are over, Sir. |
| Mix-A-Lot: | But if you don't help me, how am I going to revive my career? I need your help. |
| Me: | Okay, couldn't I just pretend to like big butts? |
| Mix-A-Lot: | Are you telling me you would say you like big butts and you could lie about it? |
| Me: | Sure. |
| | (Click) |

*Postview: This post, while funny, did not generate a large number of hits. It was still a mystery to me why "These Butts Are Big And I Cannot Lie" was so darn popular.*

## Why "These Butts Are Big And I Cannot Lie" Was So Darn Popular

I include at least one photo in each blog because experts say it increases readership especially when reposted on another site. I use officially non-copyrighted photos that are abundant on the Internet. Choosing the correct photo for this post was difficult because the subject was big, sexy butts. However, it still had to be "safe-for-work" since some people get the blog link delivered to their work email.

I chose a sort of humorous photo of a beautiful Hispanic woman with a big, round derriere. She was wearing tight, green Lycra pants and bent over so her backside filled most of the photo. One day by accident, I found out that somehow Google had linked that photo to my blog. When people clicked on the photo after a Google search, it took them directly to my blog post.

I later learned that the woman in the photo was a celebrity. Her name, Luscious Lopez, and I assumed she was an actress or singer or something.

That would have been the end the story, except one evening we had our friends Bob and Diane over for dinner and I was explaining the story of my super popular blog post to them.

That's when Diane decided to Google "Luscious Lopez" on her smart phone!

"Whoa! Did you know she was a porn star?" Diane exclaimed.

"No!," I gasped.

And that's when Diane decided to click on a link. I don't know why she did this. I wouldn't have done that. Okay, I wouldn't have done that after dinner at someone else's house.

I knew there was a big problem when I saw Diane's eyes bug out to the max.

"Oh my!," Diane yelled.

And then the sound of a very excited Miss Lopez bellowed from the smart phone. Diane quickly closed the link, but it was too late.

Bob stared at me indignantly because apparently it was my fault his wife just viewed some porn on her phone.

"I didn't know!," I strongly protested

Then I turned slowly to my wife. I had just caused Diane to play a porn video on her phone and now Bob was upset with me. I received the "wife death-ray stare". Oh, was I in trouble now!

Once again, I earnestly pleaded my innocence.

Now Bob was smiling because of how upset my wife was with me. Diane was smiling because she created the troublesome situation (at least I think that is why she was smiling …). So the evening was saved, and my guests went home happy after a delightful, entertaining evening!

My wife, however ,was not very happy. After Bob and Diane left, I was still explaining that I had not had any previous contact whatsoever (including tweets) with Ms. Lopez (who promotes herself as "The Ultimate Big Butt Latina Babe") and I had no idea how she got the nickname Luscious.

That's my story and I'm sticking to it. (I never knew that butt and I cannot lie)

# CHAPTER 4

# Sports and the Sporting Life

ATTENTION ALL NOT-SPORTS PEOPLE! PLEASE DO NOT SKIP this chapter. This is a humor book, which means I will be making fun of sports and our sports-obsessed country. Sports have become a religion in our culture and athletes are regarded as our gods. And, gods by their nature deserve to be mocked. The essays here do not contain excessive sports jargon and are intended to be enjoyed by fan and non-fan alike.

## I Don't Get A Kick Out Of Soccer

*Preview: My alma mater, The University of Akron, played for the Division I soccer championship in 2010 and this motivated me to watch an entire soccer match from beginning to end for the first time. Several of my blog posts involve my warped perceptions of trying something for a first time.*

Soccer is my least favorite of the major sports. I never played it during my athletic days and I'm not sure it even existed when I was in high school. I don't think you have to be very skilled to play it. I mean all you do is just run around and kick a ball. You learn to kick when you are still in the womb and you're running by age three. So, how difficult can it be?

I can't get serious about a sport where guys run around in shorts outdoors. In addition, I am uncomfortable with men giving cards to other men during the game. Come on; is this a tea party or a real sport?

I know soccer is currently gaining popularity in this country, but then so is socialism. I have even heard that many mothers have started playing the game. I assume that these literal "soccer moms" are attempting to lose their baby fat and fit back into their "misses" jeans and of course I support that effort.

I know that soccer is very popular in Europe, but then so is socialism (coincidence?). They take their soccer very serious over there. Often there are riots, car burnings and even deaths after a team loses an important match.

I find this very strange, because soccer is extremely boring to watch. It is not even as exciting as baseball, where between all the spitting, scratching and stepping out of the batter's box, the ball is actually only in play for a few minutes every game.

In fact, soccer is so boring that if you gave me the choice between watching a soccer match and a NASCAR race, I'll go redneck on ya. I am not a NASCAR fan because it consists of going around in circles at high speed, but never really getting anywhere, which incidentally also accurately describes my entire business career. In addition, I can't get into a "sport" where the most exciting parts are when something goes wrong and people almost die. Unfortunately, that often happens at the where I work. I don't need to see any more of that drama on the weekend.

Because of all these factors, I never thought that I would ever watch an entire soccer match. But in 2010, The University of Akron, my alma mater, played for the NCAA Division I Championship. I could only watch parts of the earlier games in the tournament before falling into a deep sleep. But I got my nachos and birch beer and planted myself in front of my big screen TV for the title match.

And I discovered something very strange about watching an entire soccer game. It is different than watching any other sport. It is very difficult to score a goal in soccer. It can take much time and effort to move the ball the entire length of the field before there is even an opportunity to score. A team can go an excruciating long time before even attempting a shot.

This wanting your team to score but having to wait so long to do so, builds up a tension that is comparable to only one other feeling known to man. And I do mean a man, not human kind. Men reading this know exactly what I am talking about and the women reading this are probably smart enough to figure it out.

This built up tension is why there is a mass orgasmic celebration when a team finally scores. It is why the announcer shouts "GOALLLLLLLLLLLLLLLLL!" It is why there is a rapturous celebration by the players. I will even condone all the male hugging that occurs, because after all, some guy has penetrated the net area and actually scored.

When guys need to score and are prohibited from doing so, bad things happen. This explains why buildings get burned, cars get torched and people die, when fans of losing soccer teams express their pent-up frustration.

This is not a unique concept. Psychologists have done many studies on how the performance of sport teams affects the sexual performance of their male fans. I remember reading about a study that found that fans of winning NFL teams had higher testosterone levels and had more sex than the fans of losing teams. This explains why the population of Cleveland, Ohio, continues to plummet. Fans of the Cleveland Browns have not had any sex in years.

Currently, The University of Akron soccer team is ranked number one in the nation this season and is expected to make a deep run in the NCAA tournament that is currently underway. Time to stock up on nachos, birch beer and ... ice!

*Postview: Unfortunately, Akron was upset early in the tournament, so fortunately I did not have to watch any more boring soccer. I did get to experience watching "my" team lose a soccer match. This did, of course, generate the same feeling a guy gets when he is rejected for sex. This is just not worth it! I have not watched more than 10 minutes of any soccer game since, and this includes the World Cup. By the way, I did not receive one angry comment from any soccer fan after this post, so I conclude soccer fans are very cool people.*

## These Are My Teams – Now Stop Laughing!

*Preview: It is really challenging to be a football fan in Northeast Ohio. I've noticed that not only do "my" teams not win many games; they have some really bizarre nicknames and mascots. Of course the people here are totally oblivious to this since we have grown up with the names and mascots all our lives, so they appear perfectly normal.*

It's football season in Northeast Ohio and this means I am cheering on my three favorite teams to victory. Okay, for two them I'm actually just yelling a lot. But I have noticed that "my" teams all have odd nicknames which warrant some discussion.

College: The University of Akron
Team Name: Zips

The team at my alma mater was originally named the "Zippers" after a new rubber boot that featured this new-fangled closure. The name had to be changed a few years later when zippers became an im-portant part of men's trousers. This would have been a great opportunity to select a new name, but no, the bad name was just shortened to Zips.

The name Zips can mean a quick movement or it means nothing, as in "you got zip". This latter meaning is very useful to headline writers whenever an Akron team gets shutout. The name also made developing a mascot difficult. If the school was true to its heritage, it would have a guy in a huge rubber boot jumping around the field. Instead a great mascot "Zippy" (a kangaroo) was created and actually was named Capital One Mascot of the Year in 2007. It could have been worse; they could have gone more generic and named the team the Akron Rubbers.

College: The Ohio State University
Team Name: Buckeyes

You might be surprised that I cheer for two college teams, but almost everyone in the state of Ohio roots for the Buckeyes. It my case I have to. The other two teams mentioned in this post have a combined 6-33 record dating back to the start of last season, so if I want to back a "winner", this is my team.

Ohio State is having a great season, but is ineligible to compete for the national championship because the team is on probation. Apparently this is due to some people valuing something called "institutional integrity" over the players being able to receive free tattoos! This is an outrage. Nothing should ever trump the opportunity to receive free tats. Come on man, it's part of the uniform!

However, "Buckeyes" is a ridiculous name. Of course the buckeye is the state nut, but why does Ohio even need an official nut? The buckeye is also inedible, which means it is a useless nut. So Ohio State fans, your team represents a useless nut. The name is laughable. No other team is named after a nut. You don't see the Arizona Almonds playing the Wisconsin Walnuts, do you?

The mascot is Brutus Buckeye, which is a tall, skinny, student running around with a huge nut for his head. Unfortunately, this resembles a ...... well ah, okay a ......, it looks like something you would see at a fertility festival. This is why you never see Brutus interacting with the cheerleaders. The cheerleaders are not allowed to hug, squeeze, or sit on top of him. And under no circumstances are they allowed to rub or kiss his head for good luck. The last time that happened, poor Brutus suffered some stiffness that lasted more than four hours and he had to seek medical attention.

NFL Team: Cleveland
Name: The Browns

There are only a few things in the world that are naturally the color brown, and most, let's say "dirt" for instance, are unpleasant (politically correct insert: this does not include people!). The team was named after Paul Brown, the first coach, but that was a long time ago. You should never name teams after people, because things change. Just imagine if a team had been named the Penn State Paternos? Paul Brown was eventually fired, so now most people believe the team is named after the color.

The name Browns makes having a mascot difficult. They tried having "Brownie the Elf", but a weak, boyish, symbol does not instill fear in an opponent. And you can't have someone running around in a long brown sock with eyeholes. This would scare the children and would risk having the mascot being continually picked up and disposed of by stadium maintenance. The sad part is that since the new Browns have returned to Cleveland they have played like brown stuff, smelly brown stuff.

Because I am a Browns fan, many people have asked me if the recent passing of the former owner Art Modell, who moved the team to Baltimore, has caused me to change my opinion of him. Of course it has. What type of callous, uncaring person do you think I am? Before, I regarded him as a bastard. Now, I regard him as a dead bastard.

*Postview: This post was written at the time of the whole Penn State scandal. I think Joe Paterno got a raw deal, but I included a joke about him anyhow because it made a point. I expected more criticism from Ohio State fans on this one since the Buckeyes are considered "sacred" by many people. I am glad they took it all in fun.*

## Have Cleveland Browns Fans Been Screwed Again?

*Preview: In April 2013, the FBI raided the headquarters of Flying J, the nation's largest truck stop chain, to investigate charges of fuel rebate fraud. No one in Northeast Ohio would have cared except that Jimmy Haslam owns both Flying J and the Cleveland Browns football team. There were fears that Haslam could be thrown in jail and the team taken from him. Browns fans at the time hoped that Haslam was the owner-messiah that would lead the Browns to Super Bowl victory.*

Cleveland Browns fans are very worried over recent events at the Flying J Corporation, which is owned by team owner Jimmy Haslam. Everyone is concerned about just how much trouble this is going to cause the team. So let's review what has happened so far.

News Item: FBI and IRS agents raid and "lock down" Flying J headquarters in Tennessee, citing issues regarding unpaid rebates.

(Now at first I thought I may have caused the problem since I had recently complained about the Flying J. A few weeks ago, the clerk at the Flying J had refused to give me my tenth cup of coffee free after I bought my first nine. He was from Florida and he claimed that there was a hanging chad on my sixth cup and thus the card showed that I had bought eight previous cups, not nine. However, the Feds said the problem had to do with diesel fuel rebates, so I was off the hook. But poor Jimmy wasn't.)

In Response Jimmy Sez: This is just a little, bitty misunderstanding. Nothing to see here. There are no rebate problems and I don't even know about any rebates, so there are no problems. See?

News Item: Everybody knew about the rebate program, including Jimmy.

In Response Jimmy Sez: Oh, you mean that rebate program? I thought you were referring to some other rebate program that I of course knew nothin' about. Yeh, there is a rebate program, but there are absolutely no problems with it.

News Item: Flying J employees say the rebate program was used to cheat and defraud customers. Rebates were promised to customers, but were not paid if not requested. They said workers commonly used the terms "jacking the customer" and "screwing the customer" in referring to the rebate program.

In Response Jimmy Sez: I ain't quittin'.

To be fair, many customers at truck stops get jacked and screwed every day. Of course this happens in the parking lot by independent contractors practicing the world's oldest profession. The big difference between these ladies and Flying J, is that at least they are screwing their customers honestly. I also doubt if they offer any rebates.

The Browns claim that the controversy will not affect the team one bit, but you know this is not true. For example, instead of preparing all weekend for the upcoming

NFL draft, Team CEO Joe Banner had to go to Dillard's department store to shop for new underwear. He reportedly blew out most of his pairs after hearing all these news items last week. Coach Chudzinski and team executive Mike Lombardi also had a few "brown outs".

The NFL is very concerned about the situation. The NFL owners don't like it if you get a speeding ticket; an FBI raid is a major faux pas. They are now extremely suspicious of a proposal that the Browns sent the league office a few weeks ago. Reportedly, the idea was to have opposing teams credit the Browns 15 points at the beginning of every game and then Cleveland would rebate the points back at the end of the game if needed. Of course, if the other team failed to ask for the rebate, lost their rebate form, or failed to fill out the form correctly and include the receipt, the Browns would keep the points. If this rebate program was in place during the 2012 season and opponents failed to collect their rebates, the Browns would have finished 14-2.

We do now know why Haslam wanted to buy the Cleveland Browns and not another NFL team. The Browns fans, customers of the team, are used to getting "jacked" and "screwed". We've been "jacked" and "screwed" so much, we hardly even mind anymore. We believe this is how the whole NFL thing works.

How much trouble are Browns fans in this time? We will know that things are extremely messed up if we hear these words in the upcoming NFL draft night: "With the sixth pick in the NFL draft, the Cleveland Browns select Defense Attorney Marvin Kammish, Harvard Law School".

Mel Kiper (NFL draft guru): Wow, what a great choice, Kammish finished third in the law class of 1993 and is great at blitzing the prosecution .....

*Postview: So far Haslam has avoided prosecution by paying huge settlements to cheated customers. However, he has been a terrible owner, making god-awful personnel choices and draft picks. The Browns still suck. So maybe it would have turned out better with Haslam in jail. He still may end up there for impersonating a legitimate NFL team owner.*

## Steroids Are Legal In This League

*Preview: Major League Baseball had been plagued for many years by players using illegal anabolic steroids to enhance their performance. The league finally started cracking down on this practice and assigning penalties in 2013. I wondered what would happen if another league took the opposite approach and actually encouraged players to use all the steroids they wanted.*

A fictional tale ….

In 2013, Major League Baseball finally decided to get tough and enacted a lifetime ban on all players who were found to be using performance-enhancing drugs. (okay, so maybe this is a fantasy tale). In response, the banned players and a group of "Mark McGwire wannabees" formed a new league, Roid Rage Baseball, and began play in 2014.

We pick up action in the fifth inning in a late season game between the Boston Biceps and the New York Needles. Skip Scary and Joe Bulk on the call:

Skip:   No outs, two on for the Biceps. The next batter is Brian Brawny, but there seems to be some delay.

Joe:    Brawny is having trouble finding a batting helmet that fits. He had been using a size 12, but it looks like he's ready to move up to the 14.

Skip: The head size has become a real issue with Brian. That's quite a melon! I really look for him to go for the home run here so he can walk around the bases.

Joe: That was really unfortunate when he got that single last night and kept tipping over when running the bases. Not only did he get tagged out, but it took two guys to set him upright.

Skip: Brawny is finally set in the batter's box and takes a 140 mph fastball high for ball one.

Joe: Brawny has recently been on a tear lately with 12 homers in his last 4 games. He currently has 140 for the season which is second in the league behind "Steroid" Sam Cooper's 155.

Skip: Brian credits his new Rawlings sports bra for his recent success at the plate. It seems his man boobs were interfering with his swing, but the bra offers all the support he needs to swing smoothly through the ball.

Joe: You can remember the commotion when the "chest" issue arose back in May when he moved up from the VX 30 to the VX 40 blend.

Skip: Yes, it got so bad at one point that his teammates refused to shower with him! Then eventually everyone moved up to the VX40. Now shower time resembles a "Girls Gone Wild" video.

Joe: Fisher fires a 120 mph curve on the corner for strike one.

Skip:   What a pitch! Does Hiller need a new mitt after that one?

Joe:    No, he's using that new Kevlar mitt. Not only can it withstand the cutter, it has greatly reduced the number of broken hands. That's great; remember that the league went through 31 catchers in its first month.

Skip:   The other thing that has really helped Brawny is that he's has grown a fully functional third eye. At first they thought it would be a third eye blind, but it's not. He now has 20-15-20 vision.

Joe:    That's high for ball two. Runners count. Do you think Wilson will try to steal third?

Skip:   No need with Brawny at the plate. And remember in June when Wilson stole third, but couldn't stop and ran straight through the wall coming to rest in the third row?

Joe:    Yes, but the team pharmacist, Jerry "The Juice" Frazier, said he dialed back Wilson's injections to three per day, so that may not be a problem now.

Joe:    Brawny swings and misses at a smoking hot fast ball that registers 157 on the radar!

Skip:   What's with Perry at first base? The guy is really scratching up a storm. I mean baseball players scratch, but this looks excessive.

Joe:    That's because he had nad replacement surgery last week. He did that pop up slide in a game against Detroit and, unfortunately, they popped out.

Skip: We have seen other players have a problem with this. The synthetic nads are great, but they can be very irritating until your body adjusts.

Joe: Fisher to the plate and, oh no, Brawny has been hit by the pitch.

Skip: That fastball registered 162 and now the ball lays shattered in front of the plate.

Joe: That's not the only thing; Brawny's forearm is laying just to the left of the batter's box.

Skip: Yes, and here comes the limb retrieval squad racing on to the field.

Joe: That is a bad break for the Biceps. Remember when Strickland suffered the same injury in May; he was on the disabled list for three weeks.

Skip: They will have to shoot him up with some CF-45: that stuff is great for healing this type of injury!

*Postview: This post has the potential to be less humorous over time if some of the former steroid users begin having serious health issues in the future.*

# CHAPTER 5

# I Love Holidays

THE HOLIDAYS, ESPECIALLY CHRISTMAS, ARE GREAT TIMES for me. I do get into the Christmas spirit which leads to some wild, wacky essays about the weird ways our culture celebrates this holiday. We deal with four holiday-oriented essays here and then four later in the book.. Because it would be difficult to read eight consecutive posts about Christmas and related subjects, especially in July. However, these posts are funny anytime of the year—so enjoy!

## A Christmas Letter To Brag About

*Preview: I hate humble Christmas brag letters. They are written for the pure benefit of the writer. The writer is able to spin the message that makes his or her family appear happy and successful and much, much superior to yours.*

*This is my personal all-time favorite post. I would write a section and then laugh out loud, then complete another and do the same. I knew that if I was cracking myself up, then I was writing something special.*

As we enter that special holiday time, one of the joys of the season is receiving those humble Christmas brag letters. Well-meaning people send these to spread Christmas cheer by raving about their perfect family and all their wonderful accomplishments that year. After reading these letters, you are devoid of all cheer, you feel that your family is inadequate, and you consider the author of the letter to be a yuletide douchebag.

Just in case you did not receive a humble Christmas brag letter this year, your Uncle Don has decided to share this year's letter from Maude, his third cousin, twice removed.

Dear Family and Friends,

Wow! Where did this year go to? I'm so sad to see it end because it's just been a fantastic year for our family! Let me share some of our stellar achievements this year:

Candi is expecting again! The good news is this time the list of possible fathers is much shorter than last year. While this shows that Candi is growing in maturity, unfortunately we will not be making a return visit to New York to be on the Maury Povich Show to "reveal" the father. Heck, we won't even need a DNA test for this one. There are only two candi-dates and they are of different, uh well, of different ancestral origins. Let's just say the winner will be clearly apparent at birth.

We are so happy that Kyle's molestation charges were unexpectedly dropped. We all knew he was innocent. His attorney said he was confident that he would have won the case in court, but the photographs he had of that young assistant prosecutor giving oral dispositions to the judge after hours really sped up the process. That attorney was expensive, but the law firm of Duckham, Buckham and Fucarelli gets results!

Todd got some interesting news at his annual checkup. It seems his prostate has swelled to epic proportions. The doctor said it is one of the largest prostates he has ever seen! It's too bad they don't have a prostate category at the county fair, or someone I know would be bringing home the blue ribbon.

Justin remains in prison, but is making tremendous strides in turning his life around and becoming a changed man. In October, he received the "Ben Dover" award for exemplary service in his cellblock!

Crystal is becoming quite the student, excelling in both science and math. The girl is spending almost all her time "in the lab". What a studyholic she is! And she is also a math whiz. So much so, that her friends have given her the nickname "Crystal Math".

Brandy got a new tattoo to add to her impressive display of body art. Unfortunately, we can't see this new one, which is amazing considering how much skin we can see! She won't reveal where it is, but it says "7-11", which I think stands for "always open".

My brother Charles, the accountant, bought himself a huge boat. He also will be getting a new job next year. Seems his company went belly up when someone drained all the money from the accounts. He is sure unlucky in that way. This is the same thing that happened at his last two jobs! Oh well, this just gives him more time to enjoy his boat. Good thing he lives on the ocean.

Kellie just got her third breast enhancement surgery. She said it was time to "trade-up". We split the cost. She paid for the actual surgery, and we paid to expand all the doorways in the house. She is also going to have to pay for the new custom-made brassieres.

Vanessa is enjoying her new job as a phone counselor. Men call her from all over the country at all hours of the day and night. She guides them through a stress relief process, and they end up learning how to relieve their own stress by taking matters into their own hands. She can do this work from home and she gets paid by the minute! Wow, getting a job like that was sure a stroke of genius.

And before I end, I must tell you about my niece Patrice who got to have a "private" meeting with one of her idols, Bill Cosby! She said it was such an overwhelming experience that she can't even remember much about it, but she said he's a real knockout.

So Merry Christmas everyone and we can only hope that 2015 is as good as this year!

Maude

And Merry Christmas Friends!

And to my Jewish, Muslim and Buddhist friends – Still Merry Christmas!

*Postview: One of my friends was reading this post and laughing hysterically. Her husband asked what was so funny. So, she handed him her tablet and then he was soon laughing, too. Her husband, who had previously met me, didn't believe I was the actual author of something this good. She assured him that I had written the post.*

*However, a week later I saw him at a basketball game. He immediately commented on how much he enjoyed the post, but then quickly added, "Did you write that?" This created mixed feelings. I was extremely pleased that he thought the post was that great. On the other hand, I was slightly offended that he thought I couldn't write that well!*

*Oh yeah, and in case anyone tries to sue me about anything, just be advised that I will be represented by the law firm of Duckham, Buckham and Fucarelli.*

## Shopping In A Winter Wonderland

*Preview: I don't go shopping at the mall very often, maybe two or three times a year. So when I do, there are so many new experiences and observations to write about. To me, it's like visiting a foreign country.*

I recently made my yearly Christmas shopping trip to the mall. This gave me a chance to experience the sights, sounds and smells of the season.

On the way to the mall, I saw a big-honking SUV with an anti-fracking window sticker. What the frack is going on here? If you are really concerned about the environment, get yourself a fracking Prius. You are either a fracking hypocrite or a fracking idiot, or both!

The Abercrombie & Fitch store was dark with strobe lights and blaring music, like a party where you just happen to buy clothes. I'm sure they have an age restriction, so I didn't go in. There was also a suffocating smell of men's body spray emanating from the store. Combine that with the thick perfume smoke pouring out of Macy's and if you have emphysema, you're not going to make it out alive. I was surprised that I did not have to step over entwined couples at the point in the mall where these two powerful sexual scents collided.

There was a new store dedicated entirely to tea. A woman offered me a sample of their new "Mango-Melon" tea, which almost made me hurl. I figure most of their customers must be hippies since they sell their tea (which is, of course, ground up leaves) by the ounce, a transaction type hippies are very familiar with. I wouldn't be surprised if some of these teas are, in fact, "smokeable".

The frozen yogurt stand had been replaced by a face and body "threading" salon. So, maybe eating all that yogurt caused people to need getting sewn back up. I have no idea what this threading entails, but it reminds me of Frankenstein. The odd thing is they do the threading right out in the open! There was a woman getting threaded right in front of me. I watched for a moment, but then I started feeling very naughty, so I quickly moved on.

I went into Macy's not really to shop, but to just to see what the successful people (or if you are so politically inclined, the rich, greedy bastards) will be wearing next year. A large, badass hat caught my eye because it was stylish and would provide coverage for my large, shaved head. However, the thing was so big I would have needed to build a new closet onto my house  just to store the thing. And, I would need to buy one of those big-honking SUVs if I wanted to wear it while driving.

The other item that I noticed was a pair of $28 red boxer shorts that had gnomes on them. This was gnome underwear, not to be confused with the Underpants Gnomes of South Park fame. The Underpants Gnomes sneak into your bedroom at night, steal your underpants, and sell them for "profit". I decided that I would not buy these because if the Underpants Gnomes found out you had gnome underpants, they would soon be making a stop at your house for sure.

My final stop was the calendar kiosk to get a 365-day box calendar for my desk. There was a large selection, but the one that first caught my attention was definitely my last choice. It came in an appropriate brown box and was titled: What Your Poo is Telling You (really exists). I do not want to correspond with my poo on a daily basis. I do not want to have to think about my poo every day of the year. Okay, let me rephrase that. I only want to think about it once a day, maybe twice, if I had Mexican. And I want my poo to remain silent, especially if I am at work.

Instead, I bought the Urban Dictionary 2013 Calendar, offering definitions of street slang on a daily basis. This is my attempt to celebrate diversity and stay relevant in an ever-changing world. To say it another way; I want to become more def in the coming year. Now don't be alarmed. I don't want to lose my "hearing" in 2013. No, according to my new calendar, I want to be in 1970's parlance, "more cool". For example: "Yo, mah pizzles, I got da hook-up at this def new club. It's suppose ta be off da hizzy."

I think next year is going to be "off da hizzy", indeed. Happy New Year readers!

*Postview: These types of posts exasperate my friend Susan. "Why are you writing about such common stuff?," she asks. "Why don't you know about these things already?"*

*And the sad answer is: I don't get out enough. With work, writing and enjoying the things I like to do, it takes up too much time. I think that's the case with many people these days. There are simply too many choices and not enough time to try them all.*

## Do The Mayans Know Something We Don't?

*Preview: This post doesn't have to do with a holiday, but a special day. An ancient Mayan calendar suddenly ended on the day December 21, 2012, and some people speculated this meant the world would end on this day. At the same time, our government had invented something called the "fiscal cliff", which if we went over it threatened to end the world also. I will let you decide which one of these is the most ridiculous. Of course I wanted to make this a good blog post because if the Mayans were correct, it would be the last one I would ever write.*

Does anybody really know what time it is?

Does anybody really care (about time)?

- Chicago

We all better hope that the answer to the first question is not the Mayans. If you haven't heard, there is an ancient Mayan calendar that ends with what is December 21, 2012, on our calendar and that has some people concerned.

I kept putting writing this blog post off and then I realized that I was running out of time. Then I realized WE MAY ALL BE LITERALLY RUNNING OUT OF TIME!!!!!!!!!!!!!!!!!!!!!!!!!!!

Now you may be wondering why I am blogging on this subject since many other writers will be covering this important event. Well, while vacationing on the Yucatan Peninsula a few years ago, I handed my credit card to the waiter after dinner and he just stood there staring at me in awe. It turns out that the name "Ake" is a Mayan name. He said I didn't look Mayan. I told him I must be one of the Germanic Mayan. The name also denotes some type of royalty, so I am  the Mayan King. Hakuna Matada! Hakuna Matada! So once again I have authority (or authoritay!) and you must respect it.

So, do the Mayans know something we don't know? They do know something special about calendars. They were good at math and understood the movement and position of the earth, sun and stars. They put this knowledge to use and were obsessed with making calendars.

They had many different calendars and unfortunately none of them included hot Mayan chicks. If they would have discovered "girls of the month", I'm sure the number of calendars would have been almost endless: "Look at the moons on Miss Second Era!" The Mayans were more concerned with counting the days rather than actually living them, which may have accounted for their downfall.

Do we need to be worried about the world ending December 21? Is there any other evidence? Junk food junkies and some fat people think the world came to an end when Twinkies recently stopped production. Some Republicans think the world ended when President Obama won re-election. And, of course, the most troubling sign of the apocalypse is that the Kardashians can make millions for simply being, well, the Kardashians.

But, there are some people, mostly dope-smoking, hippies in California that are genuinely concerned that the world will indeed end in December. I am just glad that our government is showing such great concern and responsibility by providing a calm, tranquil environment and is not talking about going over a cliff or any disaster like that.

But, I truly believe there is nothing to worry about at all. What I think happened is that one of the Mayan calendar makers finished the last "sun" cycle, which ended with the winter solstice. Coming to this break point, he stopped to get a drink and take a dump. He walked into the jungle for some privacy and was killed by a wild animal.

His teenage son was then supposed to finish the calendar, but preferred chasing hot Mayan girls and eating funny berries instead. He always told his mother he would finish the calendar "tomorrow", but he never did.

So, instead of worrying about the Mayan calendar on December 21, you should harken the words of the prophetess Annie of the Orphanic tribe, who writes:

The yellow sphere will rise high, the next cycle.

So ya gotta wait, 'til that next cycle.

Please just stay.

The next cycle. The next cycle.

I love the

Next cycle.

It's just one revolution away.

So, I am advising you all to relax and enjoy the day of December 21. Unless you are a single guy who is dating a hot Mayan chick (or really any woman) who believes that the world is actually ending on that date. Then you should by all means take the day off because you can't let this opportunity go to waste.

However, there will be a December 22, 2012. As it is written, let it be done. The Mayan King has spoken.

*Postview: My prediction was correct and the world did not end. Congress also miraculously saved us from going over the fiscal cliff. What a swell way to end the year! Because of the timeliness of the post and the huge interest in the subject, this is the third most popular "Ake's Pains" ever!*

## What Some Guys Really Want For Christmas

*Preview: Christmas commercials get a little more annoying every year. I noticed some similarities in jewelry commercials from several different companies, which indicated they were selling something other than just diamonds.*

It's that most wonderful time of the year again when those irritating Christmas commercials get played over and over until you are ready to toss your Christmas cookies. One of the magical moments of the season is when the big day finally arrives and advertisers return to selling more tolerable things such as hemorrhoid cream.

Some of the most irritating commercials are by jewelry stores. Some guy overspends for some stupid necklace,

and a joyous Christmas moment is shared
by the whole family. But these commercials
are not about what the woman wants for
Christmas, it's really all about what the guy
desperately wants.

The husband in these commercials is 30-something
with two or three younger kids and a fairly attractive wife.
Of course, the wife is busy looking after the children and she
is always tired after doing all the holiday preparations. This
means the guy isn't getting "any" and what he really wants
for Christmas is to get "some".

And, this is really what these commercials are selling.
Watch closely. The guy very nervously presents the gift to
his wife (there is a lot riding (hey, hey!) on this one). She
looks at the locket for only a second, and then looks at her
husband with an expression that he has not seen in years.
The look that says, "I want you now, you manly stud muffin!"

And then something really special happens. She em-
braces him (sometimes the feet even leave the floor) and
kisses him passionately. This happens RIGHT IN FRONT
OF THE CHILDREN! If she is this hot for the guy in front
of the kids, can you imagine what is going to happen behind
closed doors? Oh, this guy is getting some. And it's not just
"married sex" either. This is going to be some "hot monkey love". Better turn off the smoke alarm in the bedroom
because we don't want the firemen breaking down the door
and hosing us off!

And those cute children who are smiling goofily at mommy's unusual enthusiastic show of affection are in for a surprise,
too. The kids may be happy at the end of the commercial, but

five seconds after it ends, they will learn they are going to bed early tonight (like immediately) because mommy has to tend to the "Yule log".

The message is clear. The guy on the commercial bought his wife an expensive piece of jewelry and he is getting "some". If you make the mistake of buying your wife a new vacuum cleaner for Christmas, you are not getting "some". You are getting none. Although your floors may be cleaner.

Yes, I think the jewelry companies are promoting "domestic prostitution", but it must be working. If it didn't, you wouldn't see so many of these commercials year after year before Christmas. There is a connection between jewelry and sex. I'm guessing that jewelry is what most guys give their mistresses for Christmas. It's sort of like a year-end tip. It says "Thanks for letting me visit the Netherlands this year. Hope to be in Amsterdam many times next year." Monogamous guys are just hoping they can get to the Netherlands sometime over the holidays.

My message to the jewelry companies is to be more honest about what they are really selling. "Every kiss begins with ...."? Are you serious? A freaking $5 sprig of mistletoe can get you a kiss! The guy wants a lot more than that. Of course advertising that "Every (Insert your favorite euphemism here) begins with ...." would be going a bit too far.

My message to the husbands is that you are being manipulated. It might work, but if it doesn't you have spent a lot of cash needlessly. Maybe you should try another route to the Netherlands.

My message to the wives is that if your husband gives you jewelry for Christmas, he is expecting some hot sex. So please oblige. He has been manipulated by the commercials.

He has made an effort to please you. And he has spent some serious coin. So, in effect, he deserves some. However, if you have indeed been too busy and too tired to do any yule logging early in December, better to not start now. Or you could end up with a new vacuum cleaner.

Merry Christmas!

*Postview: These jewelry commercials run every year and I think there are even more of them now than in 2011 when this was posted. So they must be very effective for the jewelry companies but probably less effective for the husbands.*

# CHAPTER 6

# Fun With Economics

Attention All Economics Haters: Please read this chapter—you will find it funny. These essays are not from "Ake's Pains", but from my old economic blog. At first, the economic blog was very serious and straightforward. Then, on a whim, I started introducing some humor into the blog and my readers loved it.

Also because I used to teach economics to adult college students, I am skilled at explaining complex economic concepts in very understandable ways. So enjoy, and if you accidently learn something, all the better.

## Beware the Devil Woman

*Preview: The housing crash of 2007 was the worst housing collapse in U.S. history. I came up with an interesting story to explain how this happened, and it turned out to be surprisingly very sensual! (Note: Subprime refers to the very risky mortgages that were largely responsible for the housing crash)*

This is the story of one man's attempt at the pursuit of happiness and how it contributed to the Great Recession.

I won't forget the first time I saw her. Bleached blond hair, heaving breasts, tight jeans, packaged all so right. You couldn't miss her. I just stared at her from a distance, instantly realizing that she was oh so attractive and oh so out of my league.

I quickly passed by for a closer look when suddenly she spun around and said, "Like what you see?"

I stood mesmerized, unable to speak a single word.

"Shy, I like that," she cooed as she winked and bit down seductively on her puffy lower lip.

I still just stood there staring into her big blue eyes.

"My name's Becky, Becky Housing, and I can make all your dreams come true," she said.

"But I don't think I can afford you," I replied. "I mean, I don't think my assets are big enough to satisfy your requirements."

"Oh don't worry about that," she said. "We will try a position I call 'subprime'. It will give me all the pleasure I need and will be absolutely tantric for you."

Then she slowly slid her hand down my body and squeezed my most private part ---my wallet.

Wow! She was a prime piece of real estate and I wanted in.

It felt so good being with Becky and my net worth continued to increase all because of her. There seemed to be no limit to the heights she could take me, and it appeared to me that her assets actually grew more attractive every time that I saw her.

My friends marveled at my newfound love. I was so in love with Becky and she had told me the truth: She was making all my dreams come true.

And she was so sexy and mysterious. When we had relations, the lights were always turned off. Becky said it was better for her if I was kept in the dark. I didn't care. It was the best stuff I ever had.

I knew I had found true love and financial bliss and she kept taking my portfolio to higher and higher climaxes. I was determined to ride Becky wherever she wanted to take me.

Then it happened . . . I was at work when I heard the news. There was a report that something very bad had happened to Becky. Some sort of "crash" that was related to this subprime method.

I rushed home and there was Becky lying motionless on the floor. Her fake breasts had ruptured and fluid was pouring out of her body and streaming out the door. Likewise liquid flowed from her fake lips. The beautiful hair was really a wig that was now lying on the floor beside her. I now realized that everything about Becky had been false. And incredibly, she wasn't even a woman.

And it was even worse than that. There was this awful stench. It turns out her assets were toxic. I ran out the front door to warn my neighbors, but it was too late. To my horror, I found out that other guys on the block had been secretly involved with some of Becky's many sisters. One poor guy was involved in a threesome with Cindy Housing and Fannie Mae. He didn't even realize that Fannie Mae would give it up cheap to just about anybody.

Now there was such a stream of toxic assets flowing down the street that it even destroyed the houses of people that never were involved with Becky and her sisters. It caused a chain reaction of pandemonium. Many people lost their homes. Many people lost their jobs. Some people lost both.

If only I could have resisted the allure of Becky Housing, my life and the lives of others would be so much better now.

*Postview: Something very strange happened after this post. It received the greatest number of positive comments from women readers of all my economic posts. Because it is the most erotic essay I have ever written, it made me wonder if I should be writing soft porn instead of general humor and economics.*

## Potty Economics

*Preview: When stupid people (often celebrities) do stupid things, I find the humor in it. It is the same case when somebody writes a stupid article. (This post is from June of 2010.)*

The latest unusual economic indicator is located in your bathroom. It's toilet paper! I'm not making this up. A recent article on MSN Money says toilet paper sales can tell us much about the economic recovery.

I feel obligated to comment on this new indicator since I have written about other unusual economic indicators. But, I assure you that I will treat this subject with the seriousness and professionalism it deserves, and will resist the temptation to include any snide puns.

Some economists are flush with excitement at the possibility of a new economic indicator, but I think the argument on this one is a bit too thin to do the job. You know that the situation has hit bottom (or touched bottom) when economists are reading toilet paper instead of tea leaves. Toilet paper sales plunged in late 2008 and 2009 as the economy swirled downward. You could have knocked me right off my stool with this news. I would have theorized that toilet paper sales would be impervious to economic conditions. But, The Great Recession was so nasty, both sales and production of toilet paper went down.

Consider that there are no substitutes for this product. Corncobs or leaves might work in a pinch, but are not viable in the long term. However, many "downsized" people downsized their toilet tissue purchases. It is speculated that people went from using two-ply to one-ply and from name brand to cheaper off-brands. I knew the recession resulted in tough times, we now know it also created rough times.

There is a possibility that some people did intentionally cut back on toilet paper usage for environmental reasons. Sheryl Crow proposed in 2007 that global warming could be improved if people limited themselves to one sheet per session. Then there was the 2009 campaign from Greenpeace that claimed that our use of plush toilet tissue was destroying the environment. While I think it is important to go green, when green goes up against brown, brown usually wins. And if you want to quickly destroy an environment, imagine yourself on a four-hour plane ride with a group of Sheryl Crow disciples. (I wonder if those drop-down masks work at normal cabin pressure.)

But what makes this recession different is the amount of people that suffered a reduction of income. The unemployment rate is around 10 percent. Add in the part-time workers for economic reasons and the discouraged workers (no longer looking for work) and you are up to 17 percent of workers. Now add in the people who took a pay cut in 2008-2009, which is basically everyone in the transportation industry as well as many other hard-hit industries. Add to that nearly every commission sales person (including every real-estate agent). You need to include all waitresses and service providers whose income and tips depend on customer volume. Finally, you have many small business owners whose income is also based on volume. People who were dependent on dividend and interest income from investments also took a hit.

Run the grand total and maybe 30 percent or more of the working population suffered a drop in income. And even with the recession over, incomes are still lower than a few years ago. While most corporate pay cuts have been restored, many people in the other categories are still are trying to recover. In addition, many workers laid off in 2008-2009 have found new jobs that pay less than their previous ones.

However, the economy after being strained is starting to loosen up, and interestingly toilet paper production is up 13 percent. Toilet paper factories are being dumped on with orders and are pushing out product at a rate not seen in months. This is an indication that consumers are wiping away their economic fears and spending money again.

And now the market may be having a movement back to the other end. A new three-ply toilet tissue sold well in 2009 and continues to swell in popularity. The product's success was probably fueled by people who maintained their income levels and were looking for more comfort. Or it may just be the stress of the economy has inflamed the hemorrhoids of the nation like never before (we need some o-balm-a).

You don't need to be a bloodhound to know that conditions were smelly, and this is one paper that you didn't have to read to know things had hit the skids. I don't want to poo-poo the findings too much, but this is a trailing indicator (so lift up your shoe and remove it from the discussion). I don't believe this indicator is useful unless there is another recession of this magnitude. There are many products that followed the same sales pattern as toilet paper during this recession. It is not unique. So, I believe that we can eliminate this indicator from the discussion and start back to square one.

*Postview: One of my readers pointed out to me that after saying I was not going to resort to snide puns, I actually did!*

## Sex, Drugs and Investments

*Preview: This one actually contains legitimate advice on selecting a stockbroker, but you have to stop laughing first.*

I previously wrote that when investing you should act like a "Vulcan", using pure logic and no emotion. Based on that premise you would expect that men (kings of logic) would be much better investors than women (queens of emotion). And if you believe that to be true, you are wrong, very wrong.

A recent study showed that women hedge fund managers averaged more than 3% higher yearly returns than their male counterparts. The men tended to hold on to losing stocks too long while the women took their losses and moved the money into better places. The study concluded that testosterone may cause men to take more investment risks and to stick with loser stocks rather than to admit their mistakes. (At this point, my female readers are wondering why I had to state the obvious and my male readers are totally in denial.) It seems the presence of testosterone can cause poor investment decisions.

Now what does this "testosterone factor" mean for us average people when choosing an investment advisor or broker. Should you drop your male broker and look for a female one? Because the study is based on averages, this would be a much too simplistic approach. However, it does mean that if you are looking for a new financial advisor you should not hesitate at all in choosing a woman. And if you have two people of different genders that you regard as equal in ability, the study would say that you should pick the woman.

But men should still be careful when selecting a female broker. You do not want to be sexually attracted to her at all. The goal is to maximize the return on your assets and to do that you cannot be influenced by her assets. Be aware it doesn't matter if she achieves a 10% return on your investment, if you end up losing 50% of your net worth in divorce court. And just as you don't want your mutual fund to be "front-loaded", you don't want your financial advisor to be so either. Some guys (okay most guys) brains turn to Jell-O when in the presence of a buxom lady. No, you want your investments to be "A" rated and your broker to be "A" cupped. You see, testosterone is still a problem in this situation also.

The study does have implications for choosing male brokers and financial advisors. If you trust the study, too much testosterone is not good for making wise investment decisions. Since older men have less testosterone than younger men, this plus the experience factor should favor older advisors in general. If your broker is a young guy named "Mike Machismo", then maybe you should worry. Several of the men recently caught running Ponzi Schemes had very macho personas. And there is no riskier financial venture than a Ponzi scheme.

But now there is another problem to worry about. Perhaps you have seen the commercials warning about a condition known as "Low-T" which is short for low testosterone. Yes, now there is a prescription medicine that will quickly boost a man's testosterone. Do you understand what this means? One trip to the pharmacy could turn your mild-mannered broker Mr. Feebles into "The Tradinator": "I vill pump up ya portfolio and crush da mawket." One day your money is in a nice, stable, safer, mutual fund and the next day it could be invested in a yak farm in Pakistan.

We can't have this, so I am advocating (sounds so Obamaese) regular testosterone testing for all brokers and financial advisors. If we test athletes for steroids, we should test these people for "T" levels. And when we have this data, the investment firms can publish it along with average return rates for each broker. For example: Greg Morris has averaged a 9.3% rate of return while maintaining a "T-level" of 2.8.

I wouldn't worry too much about the T-level of your female broker unless of course she is a former member of the East German swim team. But maybe you should check for an Adam's apple just in case.

*Postview: I had actually been selected to write a weekly economic blog for a local, major newspaper's website. However, they decided to repost a few of my old blogs, (without my permission) and this post was one of them. Someone complained about the provocative language and I was quickly dropped.*

*I was upset because it was their fault for posting the past posts and they never told me I was "fired"; they just quit posting my work. However, this was an important event. To write the new blog for the newspaper, I was going to have to stop writing "Ake's Pains" due to time constraints. That would have been a major mistake, so to the hag who complained to the newspaper about this post: Thank you so much!*

## Story Time: Featuring Sammy Sublime, Billy Banker, and the return of Pooh Bear

*Preview: I have learned that even adults enjoy stories. So I often took economic concepts and turned them into the equivalent of children's stories for adults. I resist the notion to call them "adult stories".*

*This post from October 2010 explores the concept of cheap credit (partially responsible for the Great Recession), banks that were deemed "too big to fail", and government policies that favor handouts versus providing opportunities. It is impossible to write about economics without touching on politics; however, I do try to be as fair as possible.*

### Sammy Sublime Yearns for the Past

There once was guy named Sammy Sublime. Sammy lived life to the fullest. He drove luxurious sports cars; wore expensive suits; ate the finest foods, drank exotic liqueurs, smoked big cigars; and lived in a McMansion. This flashy lifestyle naturally attracted extensive female attention.

Sammy chose for his main squeeze one Valerie Vapid. Valerie was drop-dead gorgeous, a very sexy vixen. She had more curves than a calculus test and was delicious, double "D" delicious, if you get my drift, and I know you do. Sammy liked Valerie's eye-candy appeal, and Valerie liked all the things that Sammy had.

But Sammy's lifestyle was all built on cheap credit. He borrowed piles of cash to support his luxuries, and when the banks finally realized his game, they cut off all his funds. Sammy's life came crashing down. He lost his car, he lost his house, and without the bling-bling, he lost Valerie. It turns out that Sammy wasn't sublime, he was really subprime.

Sammy fell fast and hard on his way to the bottom. He then slowly began to recover and put his life back together. He lived a much simpler and modest lifestyle that matched his income. He even met a woman named Patty Plain. Patty is a very average, pleasant woman. She is a sensible match for Sammy's new lifestyle. She isn't A-List; she's an "A" cup. She isn't interested in Sammy for what he has; she is interested in him for what he is. But even though Patty is a nice woman and a perfect match for Sammy, he isn't interested in a relationship with Patty. He longs for the hot sultriness of Valerie, even though their entire relationship was based on false wealth and deceit.

## Billy Banker was Too Big to Fail

Billy Banker was too big to fail. While the other children in third grade read their assignments and did their homework, Billy watched television, played video games and engorged himself on enormous amounts of junk food. He even refused to participate in gym class. While the other children exercised and played sports, Billy just sat on his ever-expanding butt.

When the school year ended, Billy's grades were horrible. The teacher had seen many Bankers in her class over the years, but Billy's performance was exceptionally poor. Any student receiving such poor grades would not pass the class and would have to repeat the third grade, but Billy Banker was too big to fail.

Billy's poor behavior, the junk food and lack of exercise, had caused him to grow very large. He was almost too heavy for a third grade desk, so new furniture would have to be made to accommodate him. In addition, the third grade classroom was on the second floor of the schoolhouse. The floor had already started to bow under Billy's tremendous weight. If he was not promoted to the fourth grade classroom on the first floor, it was feared that Billy might crash though the floor and bring the whole school building down with him. Finally, all the junk food had festered in Billy's digestive system causing him to carry a large amount of toxic gas, which he would emit at very inappropriate times. This scared and sickened the other students. The fourth floor classroom had more windows with a better ventilation system and was better able to handle Billy's eruptions.

So the decision was made to not let Billy fail, but to help him down the stairs to the new classroom. But the principal gave Billy a stern warning. He told Billy that he needed to perform better, to study harder, and to exercise more. He told Billy that he needed to be a better Banker. To help him do that, the principal said he would enact new strict rules for Billy to make sure he improved. This made Billy very sad. Billy's face got red, he stamped his foot, and finally he turned his back to the principal and bent over. The principal quickly relented and said he was just joking about the new rules. Billy gave him a big hug and promised never to act so irresponsibly ever again. Until of course nobody was watching, and it happened again.

## Pooh Bear's New Sports Car

*(Note: This story relates to the economic stimulus of 2009-2010)*

There was a problem in the land of Nectarinia . There was a recession in the land, and the production of honey was down. However, the council in Nectarinia had a plan. The honey refinement factory was powered by a wood-burning furnace. If they could get more wood to the furnace, they could stimulate more honey production and bring the economy out of recession. So they commissioned the Grand Pooh Bear to request funds from the treasury to purchase a new wood hauling truck to carry more wood to the factory. The treasury enthusiastically supported the plan and granted a large amount of funds to the program.

Pooh Bear took the money and went to the lot to purchase the new truck, but then something went horribly wrong. Before he even looked at the truck, he saw a bright, shiny new sports car. It was wicked awesome.

"I could buy this sports car and give all my friends free rides and they would have a great time," thought Pooh Bear. "They would love me so much for the car rides that they would surely remember it when it was time to decide if I should remain the Grand Pooh Bear. And there would still be room in the trunk to haul wood to the factory."

So the Pooh Bear bought the sports car instead of the truck and spent all his time giving all his friends rides in it. He told the people of Nectarinia how great the sports car was and how happy people were to be getting the free rides. But as a result, not much wood was getting to the factory. Honey production increased, but at a very slow rate.

When the people complained, Pooh Bear told them that a new truck was needed to haul more wood to the factory to stimulate production.

"But didn't you already buy a truck for that purpose?," the people asked. "Why of course," said Pooh Bear. "What I meant to say is that we need a second truck to stimulate production."

So, Pooh Bear went back to the treasury to get funds to buy the truck. But the treasury wizards told him that there were no more funds available for a second vehicle and he would have to make do with the one he had. And so the honey production slowly dripped ahead and the recession continued.

*Postview: I bet you thought economics couldn't be this fun. That's why my economics students gave me high marks on evaluations!*

## My Poets Have Never Been Cowboys

*Preview: This post is from March 2011.*

Recently, Senate Majority Leader Harry Reid (D-NV) defended maintaining the funding of the National Endowment for the Arts. His best argument for continuing the funding was that if the funds were cut, the Cowboy

Poetry Festival (held in his home state of Nevada, what a surprise) might have to be cancelled.

Unfortunately, I am not making this up. We (taxpayers) are subsidizing cowboy poets and powerful people in government think it would be tragic if we stopped providing this service. Isn't it interesting that you would get the same reaction from a junkie if you threatened to take away his smack.

I think that if I needed an example of why cutting the funding was needed; I might play the "cowboy poetry" card. If we do go broke, 100 years from now people will say, "Look at those idiots. The deficits were so high, but they still spent money on that cowboy poetry."

What is cowboy poetry anyway? When I told my friend Sue that I was going to write on this subject, she said that it wouldn't be fair to comment on it without actually reading some of it. She is obviously an intelligent woman, so I did read some cowboy poetry using a new technology called the "Internet".

It is bad. It is "the last thing I would read in the doctor's office" bad. It is "Oprah reading list runner-up" bad. It is "against the Geneva Convention to read this to prisoners" bad. It is "third-grade poetry contest" bad. I had to clean my computer monitor after the download to get the stench out.

But if it so bad, why do cowboys continue to write it, and why is there a taxpayer-funded festival every year to promote it? My theory is that cowboys do this stupid thing for the same reason men have done stupid things throughout the ages: Chicks dig it.

And there is another dynamic taking place here. Woman love cowboys. They find this rugged masculinity very sexy and appealing. Why do you think so many men's colognes have "western" names? Even business executives want to smell like cowboys, because woman love cowboys. If you can't be a cowboy, the next best thing is to splash on some Stetson and smell like one.

Even gay men are attracted to cowboys. My evidence is the cowboy character in The Village People and the movie Brokeback Mountain. So if you like men, you like cowboys.

And when cowboys write poetry, they reveal their sensitive side. And guys know that women crave that mix of strength and sensitivity. Of course, most guys who realize this still have problems making it work.

Woman: "What the hell are you doing?"

Man: "I'm trying to be strong."

Woman: "Well stop it and try to be more sensitive, you jerk!"

The next day …

Woman: "What the hell are you doing?"

Man: "I'm trying to be sensitive."

Woman: "Well quit being a wimp and show some strength!"

So, I'm not surprised that cowboys write poetry. I'm also not surprised that a cowboy poetry festival is popular as hundreds of cowgirl wannabees descend upon northern Nevada (including maybe some Vegas showgirls). For a weekend, the cowboys have more groupies than rock stars. Sure, they are saddle sore for the next week, but they don't mind. It wouldn't even surprise me if a cowboy poet first coined the term for that reverse riding style.

So yes, I guess cowboy poetry has a purpose. And yes, I suppose people have a great time at the festival. But I still don't understand why one dime of taxpayer money should go to fund this. If the cowboys are having as much fun as I think they are, they will most assuredly pay all the expenses.

So in honor of cowboy poetry, I will end this blog with a cowboy poem of my own:

> Them chaps are rubbin' me the wrong way
> Them chaps are ruinin' my day
> Them chaps in D.C.
> Are really irritating me
>
> Them chaps are chaffing my thighs
> And tellin' us lies
> They take corn for my cattle
> To make gas for Seattle
>
> Them chaps are pinching my buns
> And they're after my guns
> They don't want to hear
> Then they go taxin' my beer
>
> Them chaps are inflaming my loins
> As they grab all them coins
> They're taxin' my smokes
> And screwing us folks
>
> Them chaps are grinding my nubs
> And sayin' things that are dumb

Thar dense as a bird
And make more manure than my herd

Them chaps are rubbin' me the wrong way
Them chaps are ruinin' my day
Them chaps in D.C.
Are really irritating me

Yee Haw!

*Postview: I would hope you do not want your taxes used for cowboy poetry, no matter what side of the political fence you sit on!*

# CHAPTER 7

# On The Home Front

I LIVE IN AN OLDER ALLOTMENT IN AN AFFLUENT SUBURB. At one time I could see buffalo from my house before the herd was sold off, yet I am a five-minute drive to the Home Depot. It is typical suburbia in the Midwest.

Now that I work from home, I naturally write more about "home" stuff because I see and experience more things here. This chapter features neighbors, dogs, grass and lots of leaves. Enjoy.

## Why Owls Are Better Than Viagra

*Preview: I love working from home. There are much fewer distractions than working in an office. However when there are disruptions, they are much more irritating than normal. And harder to fix.*

I was busy working away at my computer in my home office early on a Tuesday, when suddenly …

Rat-tat-tat  Rat-tat-tat  Rat-tat-tat  RAT-TAT-TAT-TAT-TAAAAAAAAAAAAAAAT!

"What the heck is that?," I thought. The loud, mind-numbing noise stopped for a while, but then periodically returned.

I looked out the window almost expecting to see a road worker with a jackhammer, but nothing. A house up the street had recently advertised auto repairs and I thought it could be an air wrench.

The noise stopped later in the morning and I could finally work in peace. But the next morning about the same time, Rat-tat-tat Rat-tat-tat Rat-tat-tat RAT-TAT-TAT-TAT-TAAAAAAAAAAAAAAAAT!

This time it sounded as if the noise was coming from right above me. I ran outside, but as soon as I got to the corner of the house, the noise suddenly stopped. I repeated this process several times that morning. However as soon as I got to the same spot, silence.

Something evil was happening on my roof, but what?

The next morning the racket returned eerily about the same time. But this time I quietly slipped out the door at the other end of the house and moved stealthily like a ninja (okay like a tall, fat, middle-aged ninja) and approached the roof from the other side of the house. It was then I caught the culprit red-handed. Or should I say I caught him redheaded? Sitting right above my window was a redheaded woodpecker, pecking the hell out of my roof. I made eye contact with the bird. He looked angry, but not as angry as I was.

Stupid pecker. Stupid, stupid pecker, I thought.

The morning peckings continued. It was very difficult to work with the pecker frequently going Rat-tat-tat Rat-tat-tat Rat-tat-tat RAT-TAT-TAT-TAT-TAAAAAAAAAAAAAAAT! right above my head at random times every morning.

This was ironic. For many years, I had to deal with stupid peckers at work. Some of these peckers had the title of director, some of them vice president, and yes, some of them I even called "boss". Now I was no longer in an office, but was instead working from home, and I still had to deal with a stupid pecker.

But why was this stupid pecker hammering on my roof every morning? Of course I complained to my wife about it.

"I know why the woodpecker is doing this", she explained. "He's mad because you stopped feeding him".

I initially thought this was ridiculous. Who is she, the bird whisperer?

I had been putting out corn, seeds and nuts for the birds and squirrels during the brutal winter. This had attracted a significant number of cardinals, blue jays, and yes, woodpeckers to my deck. The power pecking had begun the week after I had stopped the daily, morning feeding. The racket always started just about the time I put the feed out and the birds would show up for breakfast. Somehow that hungry pecker had figured out the exact spot in the house where I worked and was pounding the hell out of the roof right above me.

This wasn't a stupid pecker! This was a nasty, intelligent, savant-type of pecker, and boy was he pissed at me! This was the equivalent of an angry customer pounding his fist on the counter. I was playing a real-life version of Angry Birds.

I was not about to give into this pecker intimidation and resume the feedings, but the morning peckings continued. This was until the stupid pecker let loose early one Saturday morning awakening my wife. Like many problems in my home, they persist until my wife gets upset and then things happen. That afternoon she went shopping and returned with two large, expensive, fake, plastic owls, which were intended to scare away the woodpecker. She placed the owls at opposite ends of the house.

I thought this was the most ridiculous idea ever. I was not happy about these expensive forgeries at all. This pecker was surely smart enough not to be fooled by ludicrous fake owls. But very soon after that, the peckings stopped.

So what did I learn?

Woodpeckers hate owls.

Owls dominate woodpeckers.

Stupid peckers, wise owls.

Stupid husband, smart wife.

If only I would have known about this sooner, I would have gladly taken an owl to work with me to scare away all those nasty peckers I encountered over all these years.

And so concludes the story of how my wife getting two large fake plastic hooters took care of my pecker problem.

*Postview: I would never have imagined this trick would have worked, but I have no other explanation. I only include my wife in my blog if it makes her look intelligent or it makes me look stupid. She then enjoys reading my posts very much.*

## It's Hard To Sit On This Fence

*Preview: Let's consider this story fiction based on fact. The fact part is that most of the leaves from my neighbor's huge oak tree end up in my yard. I did consider buying a temporary fence to prevent this, and then my imagination just ran wild!*

My next-door neighbor Jose has two very large oak trees in his front yard. In autumn, he waits for all the oak leaves to fall from the trees and then he hires a lawn service to clean his yard.

While this works great for Jose, it works badly for me. My yard is downwind from his, which means most of the oak leaves end up blowing into my yard. You would think that the leaves would continue to travel through my yard into the street, but life isn't fair and the leaves seem to stick like Velcro® to my grass. Unfortunately, I don't use a lawn service for my leaves. I don't use a blower. I don't use a mower. I use a contraption that consists of a long wooden handle with long metal prongs at the end. It is commonly referred to as a "rake".

But this year I had a great idea. A quick trip to the local hardware store and for less than $20 I had a short, white garden fence. I quickly installed the fence at the edge of my property and waited for the leaves to begin falling.

I watched in glee as those leaves smacked hard against my fence and then fell stunned back into Jose's yard. A few "high fliers" made it over, but my yard was basically leaf-free while his yard was feeling the "full brunt of autumn".

I thought the fence was working very well until one day I was confronted by an angry Jose.

"What is the idea with this fence?," he asked. "There are too many leaves in my yard and there is no place for them to go."

"But those are your leaves", I pleaded. "They are your problem and you should deal with them, not me."

"The leaves should have the right to go wherever they want and they like your yard. They are very happy there. That is why they stay and do not come back," he stated.

"When your leaves settle in my yard, I have added work and expense to tend to them. That should not be my responsibility, it should be yours." I protested.

"This is not right," said Jose. "You are a bigot because you do not like oak trees and do not want their leaves in your yard."

"Not true," I said. "I do not want maple leaves. I do not want birch leaves. I do not want any leaves that do not belong in my yard!"

Jose shouted, "You are not being a good neighbor," and stormed back into his house.

I thought the issue was settled until Halloween evening when I heard a voice booming from a loud speaker from Jose's yard. I ran outside and I saw a very strange scene. There was Jose's son standing on his porch, dressed in a suit, wearing a Ronald Reagan mask and speaking into a microphone. Furthermore, there were chairs set up in the yard and all the neighbors had apparently been invited to attend this presentation.

I thought this was just some Halloween fun. The kid was really doing a good job imitating Reagan; he was doing the head bob and everything. He was reciting an actual Reagan speech and was really getting into it. I had just realized this was Reagan's Brandenburg Gate speech delivered near the Berlin Wall in 1987, when suddenly he turned and looked right at me, and proclaimed: "Mr. Ake, tear down this wall!"

"It's not a wall, it's a fence," I yelled.

But it was too late, all hell broke loose. All the neighbors started arguing with each other. Some thought it was wrong to put up the fence and contain the leaves. Others said the fence was a great idea. One guy thought I didn't need the fence and that I should just buy a blower and blow all the leaves back into Jose's yard. I ran back into my house and peeked out my window until the commotion calmed down.

Who would have thought that a simple solution involving a fence could cause so much controversy?

*Postview: This post was from October 2011. I probably would not write it today since it seems as a society we are losing our ability to laugh at anything mildly political. I included it here because it is clever and I still think it is funny no matter what side of this "fence" you are on.*

## Dancing On The Grave Of A Dead Dog

*Preview: I truly do not know the real name of this neighbor. I got the term "Numbnuts" from a former co-worker Joe who would assign derogatory nicknames to people he disliked. And once that moniker was applied, he would stick with it. This caused the rest of us in the office to have to remember who was who. So when Joe said Fartface had rejected his proposal, we would know he really meant Pete in Accounting.*

My neighbor Numbnuts had a huge, mean dog that would attempt to kill me when I did my frequent exercise walks. The dog is a mixed breed, a combination of Rottweiler and bear. It would growl and lunge aggressively at me. It would even attack my car when I drove by. I hated this dog and it hated me.

I refer to this guy as Numbnuts not because he has nerve damage in his man parts, but because he has damage in his brain parts. He could not control this beast on its leash. The monster dog just pulled Numbnuts all over the road. Numbnuts would yell frantically for the dog to obey with this wide-eyed, stupid look, but the dog would never obey.

This caused a big problem in that Numbnuts would often walk Cujo after dark, in the street, with no flashlight. (The allotment has no sidewalks or streetlights). And since the dog was in effect walking Numbnuts, this created a dangerous situation.

Because Numbnuts could not control this hellhound and I feared the monster-mutt could snap its collar, escape, and proceed to maul me, I had to avoid them on my walks. This was a major inconvenience. Because there is only one way out of the neighborhood, sometimes I had to wait for them to clear the area or even return back to my home for safety.

So I allowed Numbnuts and Damien to rule the streets, until one fateful night.

I had just driven into the allotment one night when I had to suddenly swerve to avoid hitting the mutt. The dog had decided to sit right in the middle of the road and there was Numbnuts, with his dumb Numbnuts expression, frantically pulling as hard as he could on the leash, but to no avail. As I swerved, Numbnuts yelled at me to slow down. But I was not speeding.

As soon as I had straightened my car out of the turn, they appeared in my headlights and I veered to the right narrowly missing the dog. I had not even had time to accelerate. I stopped the car, lowered the window, and yelled at him to "Get a flashlight". And that's when Numbnuts fired an "F-bomb".

Now he is an idiot, doing something idiotic, and he somehow thinks this is my fault. Of course I am fizzed. I put the car in park, unbuckle the seat belt and reach for the door. It is at this point I realize I will not only be confronting Numbnuts, but the demon monster dog from hell, the dog that wants to kill me. I put the car in drive and continue home. Well played Numbnuts, well played.

But you don't fizz me off this bad without consequences. So, I decided to "take back" the streets. I needed protection, but what type? My machismo-oriented, NRA-type friends suggested I conceal carry. This however would pose a problem in the summer when walking with very little clothing would only leave me one obvious area for concealment. I don't want the women in the neighborhood ogling the size of my Luger. It may be fully loaded, but I am not that well cocked (we are still talking guns here). Concealing a weapon in this manner also makes premature ejection a very painful experience.

I considered an electronic dog repellent device but at the moment of truth with demon dog a few feet away, I did not want to trust my life on a gadget that I could not see or hear. I envisioned someone at the morgue saying, "No Jeff, we are still not able to get that device out of his hand. He was still pushing that button really, really, hard right to the end.

I settled on a canister of dog mace. The drawback here is if I unload a blast of mace at the dog, I could also inadvertently gas Numbnuts. ... Okay, so there really are no disadvantages with using the mace.

I do admit I felt some machismo walking down the street with my new weapon. I wanted the chance to confront this enemy. I wanted to have a Dirty Donnie moment where I stared him down and uttered, "Go ahead pooch, make my day." I wanted to see the fear on Numbnuts face when I didn't leave the street, when I stood my ground, and confronted them.

But alas, I carried the mace for months and even though I would occasionally see Numbnuts with the dog, there never was a confrontation. Then, I stopped seeing the dog altogether.

Ding dong, the wicked dog was dead. Ordinarily I would be sad when a beloved dog died, but not in this case. This dog hated me and wanted to kill me, and now it was dead. I wanted to literally dance in the street, but I refrained knowing my bad dancing ability would alarm the neighbors. I felt great. I felt euphoric. I felt liberated. Hallelujah, the streets were safe gain.

But now Numbnuts has a new dog. And in a moronic case of pure numbnutsian logic, he has found a dog of the exact same mix. Cujo, Jr. has arrived. Of course I discovered this one night driving home when I turned the corner and was startled by Numbnuts standing on the road; leash in hand, no flashlight.

The dog is a now a "puppy", more like a mini-monster. It has already looked at me with disdain. I am sure it is eager to grow large enough so that it can kill me. I know it hates me and I hate it already. My joy is gone, I am depressed ..... Numbnuts has a new dog. Where did I put that mace?

*Postview: Yes, I am carrying the mace again because unbelievably the new dog is dumber and meaner than the old dog. Four months after I posted this I was driving up the street when I saw the dog running down a hill, full speed, headed right in front of my car. (He had gotten loose and apparently Numbnuts was unaware of this, surprise!)*

*I brake hard (wasn't going very fast, had just left my drive-way) and hope the dog made it past, but then I hear the "thunk". It is the first time I have ever hit a dog. I gasp, then sigh, but before I can get out of my vehicle, the dog jumps up and runs up the street, scared and favoring his right side.*

*I then continue to the intersection where I see the dog running back to his home on the right, as I turn to the left. As I continue driving, I replay the scene in my head and realize something important. I had brought my SUV to a complete stop a second before impact. I had not hit the dog, he had hit me!*

*Yes, this fool dog had run down a hill full speed, right into my relatively new vehicle. My main concern then was if there was damage to my car. Fortunately, there was not and the dog has since recovered. I think Numbnuts has the perfect pet – dumb owner, dumb dog. Somehow I don't think this story is over.*

## The Grass Cannot Be Greener On The Other Side

*Preview: An insight to the weird happenings that go on inside my head. The stuff that bothers me at night before I fall asleep....*

I can remember back when I thought people who used lawn treatment services were idiots. I mean who would actually pay someone to fertilize their yard when it was so easy to do yourself? Spending gobs of money just to have the best looking yard on the block? What morons!

But then those yearly trips to the hardware store became less enjoyable. This was mainly because the bags of weed-and-feed mysteriously became heavier every year. Why they decided to start making the bags harder to lift, I'll never know.

So a few years ago, I actually started employing a service to treat my lawn. This change meant the condition of my lawn suddenly became of supreme importance to me. I had made an investment in my yard, and I could literally watch that investment grow.

Of course, they put that little flag in your yard after they finish. They tell you the flag is to warn people your lawn has just been treated, but of course that is not the real reason. In reality, the flag symbolizes your commitment to a superior lawn. It states that your lawn is so much better than the surrounding turf, that it deserves its own flag! As I stand in my yard, hands on my hips, I am declaring independence for the Kingdom of Donrovia! Long live the king! Of course as referenced previously, my neighbors are thinking, "What a moron. He's wasting good money on his stupid lawn."

But this year, something very disturbing transpired. I noticed in June when I looked out my bedroom window that my lawn did not look any better than the widow Cooper's next door. How could this be? I'm paying hundreds of dollars to have the best lawn on the block and her lawn looks as good as mine? I speculate that my lawn service has provided substandard treatment. I am perplexed and upset.

A few days later while walking my dog, I solved the mystery. At the other end of the widow Cooper's yard was a flag. It was a flag from another lawn service. That witch had gotten her lawn treated for the first time since I moved in. How dare she! This was totally unacceptable. This was an outrage.

Then to make this incredibly bad situation even worse, upon further investigation I discovered something that almost made my head explode. The widow Cooper's yard actually looked better than mine. This pushed me over the edge. So I called my lawn service to complain.

| | |
|---|---|
| Me: | My neighbor uses a competitor's lawn service and her lawn looks better than mine. |
| Lawn Guy: | How is it better? |
| Me: | Her color is more vibrant. |
| Lawn Guy: | So are you actually saying that the grass is greener on the other side of the fence? |
| Me: | No, what are you talking about? There is no fence, but yes, her grass is in fact greener. |
| Lawn Guy: | Well it always will be … |
| Me: | That's what I'm trying to tell you. Yes, it always is. Monday, Tuesday, whatever. On all days that end in "y". Her grass is greener. So you agree with me? |

| Lawn Guy: | No, the grass always appears greener on the other side of the fence. |
|---|---|
| Me: | Alright, I told you before, there is no *!#&ing fence! And I am shocked at your lousy attitude. You are conceding that your competition always does a superior job! Dude, show some pride in your work. If you're going be like that, maybe I should use those guys next year! |
| Lawn Guy: | No, it's an expression. It is an optical illusion. Her grass only looks greener because at a distance the colors appear stronger. I assure you the grass is the same color. If you looked at it from her yard, your grass would appear greener. |

Of course I thought his explanation was pure bull crap. I considered sneaking through the woods across the back of the property to look across the widow Cooper's yard into mine to see if what the lawn guy told me was true. However, I realized I would then be standing in the yard of my neighbor "Hot Carla" with a good view of her bedroom window. If I got caught trespassing by the police, I would have to convince them I had snuck over there to get a peek at the widow Cooper's grass and not Hot Carla's ass.

If it went to trial, not even Perry Mason could save me:

| Prosecutor: | I now present Hot Carla, and we are going to label this evidence Exhibit A ....... and uh, B. |
|---|---|

| Perry Mason: | Wow! My client confesses your honor. Tom, you are so guilty. |
| Me: | My name is Don, not Tom! |

So instead of sneaking over there, I took a photo on the property line and as you can plainly see the grass is truly greener on the left side of the stick (my neighbor's side).

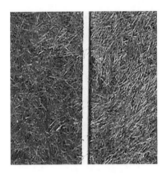

The widow Cooper has plainly kicked my grass. Her lawn company has pumped up the nitrogen and has defeated my kingdom.

I am dejected. I know I should not be this worried about the condition of my grass, and I shudder to think what may happen the next time the neighborhood kids venture on to my cherished investment.

*Postview: I didn't really call my lawn service to complain – but I did consider it. Now aren't you glad that you are not me?*

## Ode To A Broken Rake

*Preview: My first try at "real" poetry. I started attending meetings at a local writer's guild. I figured if I wanted to be a legitimate writer, I may as well hang out with some. My good friend Owen*

*reads his poetry all the time at the meetings, so I think he may*
*have inspired me to write this one.*

My yard lay buried beneath autumn's final fury
Covered in leaves, mountains of leaves
The tundra gasping and choking for oxygen
And this was not even of my making
The dreaded giant oak next door had rained down its
    closing blast
Dead matter everywhere, decaying foliage
Now festering and rotting in a heap upon my lawn

I went to fetch my rake to eradicate this awful mess
I looked, but could not find it anywhere
When I inquired about the location of my tool
I was told that the rake was
    broken
That the tines had fractured
    and fallen off
I shed a tear that my trusted
    friend was gone
That it had died, no longer
    useful, discarded so abruptly

I did not inquire why a new rake had not been
    procured
A bright, shiny one with new strong tines
Perhaps there were hopes the leaves would all blow
    away
That they would all magically float to someone else's
    place

But now I am powerless to rid myself of this disgusting mass of filth
Because my rake, my rake, is broken
It has no tines, the tines have all fractured and fallen
off

I can hear the leaves now mocking me
"You had planned to gather us all in bags and
burn us"
"But now you can't, because your rake is broken"
"It has no tines, the tines have all fractured and fallen
off"
"You thought you could dispose of us with ease"
"But even though we are dead, yet we live"
"Viva la resurrection and viva la revolution!"

Ha! A true leaf "movement" would have them moving
off my yard
A real "uprising" would be up rising and landing
somewhere else
This was more like a "sit in" that I was powerless to
stop
My property was being taken over by plant-based
radicals
They had the upper hand and they shall not be moved
Because my rake, my rake, is broken
It has no tines, the tines have all fractured and fallen
off
I stand there, my head hung in shame
All the other yards are free of leaves, pristine,
beautiful

Because the neighbors cleaned their plots using rakes
Rakes that were unbroken, rakes with tines that are
    intact
I waited 'til the stubborn oak had played is final card
It is tyranny, egregious tyranny, I tell you
My domain is held captive and I am helpless to free it

Perhaps someone would be kind enough to loan me
    their rake
They had no need of it because their leaves are all gone
I will just explain to them that my rake is broken and
    it has no tines
I knock feverously at their doors, but no one answers
But I persist because winter approaches and the leaves
    are many
And my rake, my rake, is broken
It has no tines, the tines have all fractured and fallen off

I cry out, "Please kind sir, my yard is full of dead, de-
    caying leaves"
"My grass is suffocating and perishing underneath this
    deathtrap"
"My rake is broken and it has no tines"
"The tines have all fractured and fallen off"
"Please, please, I'm begging you"
"Have mercy on, have mercy on me!"
"Let me borrow your rake so I may clean my yard"

My pleas are met with silence, no one will help me
They are at home, but they are fearful I will fracture
    their tines

Then their rake would be broken also and they would
    be as pathetic as I
I return to my house rakeless, to the laughter of the
    leaf commune
I fall to my knees, shake my fist, and wail loudly
Because my rake, my rake, is broken
It has no tines, the tines have all fractured and fallen
    off

*Postview: Literally I was told: "the rake has no tinges". Using tinges would have made it made it funnier, but it is the wrong use of the word. I did not want to be flooded with email from linguists and English teachers.*

## You Will Not Be Offended By My 100th Post

*Preview: I do admit that I am oversensitive to criticism of my blog. I react the exact same way as I do to criticism of my off-spring. However, most of the time, the negative comments are rather humorous. When sent to the blog itself, I will post almost all critical comments and most people get an extra chuckle out of them. I am pleasantly surprised that I don't receive more critical comments than I do. Most people "get it"; I feel some sadness for those who don't.*

This post marks the 100th edition of "Ake's Pains" (if we don't count the three "serious" posts). The blog debuted in May 2011, and I can't believe the number of readers it has and the number of hits it has received. So I would like to sincerely thank all my readers who enjoy this blog.

However, everyone is not a fan of the blog. Recently, I received a long message from a young woman named Frances who had seen the blog on a social networking site where I repost it. She found the blog very boring and somewhat (gasp) offensive and couldn't understand why people would have any interest in my personal, mundane stories.

The problem is many women under 30 years of age don't get my jokes. It's not that they are stupid. Humor is subjective and they don't comprehend it. And that's okay; not everyone gets or enjoys my stuff. I'm not surprised Frances was bored by my blog; however there are four very disturbing things about her message:

1. Even though she was bored and offended, she read the entire lengthy post. With the thousands of articles available on the Internet each day, who has time to read the bad ones? Then she writes me a long message to tell me why she was bored. Either she has too much free time or too little life.

2. This particular post was not offensive. You would have to try to be offended by it, which evidently she was successful in doing. Because she did not get the jokes, she thought I was stating serious opinions.

3. She thought I should not repost any more blogs. Apparently she also has time to police the Internet. My brilliant solution was to suggest that she not read any more of my posts, but allow other people to enjoy them.

4. She goes by the name "Frances". Enough said.

However I do care about Frances and the young women like her who wish to read blog posts by middle-aged studs like myself without being offended and made sad. So I am dedicating this 100th post to Frances by offering the least offensive story that I can possibly write.

## Don's Swell Day

I awoke in the morning after getting the recommended seven hours of sleep. Sleeping less would be unhealthy and sleeping more would be slothful. I then showered and ate breakfast.

Before starting the workday, I spent time in my executive bathroom. It was a productive session because I had been careful to ingest the recommended daily amount of fiber the day before. I followed Sheryl Crowe's suggestion and used only one sheet of toilet paper. I didn't feel very fresh, but we all have to do our part to save the planet.

I then started my workday. I do work at a "for profit" company, but I made sure that my actions did not produce too much profit because that would be greedy and might lead to creating more poor people.

At lunchtime, I had a sammich. I made my own sammich and at no time did any females participate in the making of this sammich. The sammich consisted of tofu and sprouts on gluten-free bread. I know eating tofu could increase the size of my man-boobs, but we must all sacrifice to save the planet. Plus, this helps me reach my daily fiber goal.

After lunch, I decided to take a power walk to fulfill my daily physical fitness goal. It was a very hot day so I expected to burn a lot of calories. As I started down the street, I saw my neighbor, Hot Carla, washing her car in her string bikini.

I thought about engaging her in some friendly, neighborly small talk. Perhaps I should stay and offer to hose her down if she gets overheated. But no, she was busy scrubbing that car very vigorously, so a friendly wave will have to do. I resume the walk, but for some reason have problems taking a full stride.

When I get to the top of the hill, I notice Mr. Hairy Spider on the edge of the road. I don't want him to get squished, so I gently pick him up and carry over to a safe place. Ahhh,  Mr. Spider really likes me. He has such a tight grip on my finger it's difficult for me to set him free. Have a good day Hairy!

On my way back I notice Hot Carla has really worked up a sweat! That bikini is soaked! It's wax time and she is buffing the heck out of that car, but my attention is diverted to the other side of the street where Mister Squirrel is frolicking and storing food for the winter. Bury those nuts Mr. Squirrel. Bury those nuts!

I return home and complete my workday. I work hard, but not too hard, lest I become rich and evil. I feel a little guilty about making too much money, so at the end of the day I write some checks to some caring charities in order to save the planet.

I have dinner consisting of organic, free-range vegetables and a big heaping helping of quinoa. I then relax by watching PBS because it has programs unavailable on the other 3,000 channels. Tonight's program is "Mating Habits of the Squid". It is interesting, but I do cover my eyes during the "good" parts. I distract myself by thinking about how shiny Hot Carla's car must be after all her scrubbing and buffing.

At bedtime, my hand is really swollen, my bum is on fire and my loins are still tingly, but all in all, it has been a swell day!

*Postview: The criticism was directed to the post "Father of the Bride" (the post appears in Chapter 11). This post is very inoffensive. Yes, it does point out that men and women experience and prepare for a wedding differently. If you have a problem with that, you are going to have a problem with life. But it produced a great blog post and people loved my irreverent response to political correctness.*

# CHAPTER 8

# Working It

M Y LAST "OUTSIDE OFFICE" (I NOW WORK AT HOME) COULD have produced enough material for weekly blog posts. Of course that did not have happen. I would have been fired after the first post because corporations have no sense of humor. If a corporation were a person, he would be a bastard. Almost all corporations are bastards. That is why they hire bastards to be executives. Someday, I plan to write an entire book on what strange things happen in the workplace. Most of this chapter contains stuff that has happened in the last two years since I started working from home, with two essays from the distant past.

## It's Sexual, But It's Not
## Always Harr(ass)ment

*Preview: This post is from November 2011, and at that time several sexual harassment cases were in the news and people were vigorously debating the issue. Since people were talking about it, I decided to share some of my experiences throughout my career. And yes, these stories are true. Some people thought I made them up or enhanced them, in these cases there was no need to.*

Sexual harassment is back in the news so it is an appropriate time to address this important subject. I thought about including this first story when I wrote the blog posts about pink shirts, but ran out of space.

The shirt connection is as follows: A few years ago, I was passing a female coworker in a remote stairwell when she looked at me and said, "I just want to rip that shirt right off your body".

I was taken aback since I really didn't know how to respond. If she liked my shirt, "Nice shirt" would have been sufficient. I wasn't sure if she was interested in me or my shirt, and the thought of me standing there bare-chested while she made love to my shirt (my shirt's too sexy for my bod, too sexy for my bod...) was not very appealing to me.

So, I just said "thank you" and quickly moved down the stairs. She was a chunky, spunky little monkey, and I was really unsure what was going to happen next and did not want to find out.

This was technically "sexual harassment". To determine this, you just reverse the scenario. If I tell the buxom secretary that "I just want to rip that sweater right off your body", I'm soon going to be meeting with the HR department and it will not be pleasant.

But in reality it is very difficult to actually harass the average male. I say average, because the "pretty boy", studly types can be harassed. I would expect that being continuously propositioned by ugly hags would be unnerving, and maybe having your butt repeatedly grabbed would eventually get old, but I know nothing about that. Of course, any type of supervisor-subordinate harassment no matter what the sexual dynamics, is very legitimate and serious.

But even as an average-looking guy, I have been subject to around 20 incidents over my career that could be regarded as sexual harassment in the workplace. These include three cases involving physical contact and four instances involving raised skirts. Of course I did not report any of these acts because I never felt threatened and it was never persistent. Almost always, I considered the incidents (like the shirt story) very humorous.

The funniest incident was when an attractive female co-worker wearing a very short skirt walked into my office, walked around behind me, and sat on my desk right beside me with her legs slightly spread. That's right, my face was just inches from her hooha and combined with the short skirt, she was definitely in violation of the "stripper laws" in Utah.

And then she actually expected me to engage in a business discussion sitting there with her skirt just barely covering her "naughty bits". This was impossible however because a man's brain totally shuts down in this situation. She's like: "I think we should use this program to track the project blah, blah, blah ..." The brain just hears "Hooha, Hooha, HOOHA" (imagine a loud donkey bray).

It was one of the most physically uncomfortable positions I have ever experienced in my career. I couldn't move backwards because that would give me an unobstructed view of the hooha. I couldn't move sideways because it was a three-sided desk. It hurt my neck to look up at her from that angle and if I looked down there were just legs and hooha.

So I keep my head level which then resulted in me looking straight into her more than ample chest. My office had a glass wall so everyone who walked by could see this situation and several guys kidded me about it later.

Another very humorous incident happened at an off-site company Christmas party. I was standing in the buffet line behind my best (platonic) female friend in the office (my "work wife"). Suddenly she unexpectedly starts rubbing her booty against my crotch. This would be outrageous enough on its own, but what made this really special is that our spouses were standing nearby in the same line!

Once again, I was trapped. I couldn't suddenly jump out of the line. I couldn't yell for her to stop without attracting attention. Eventually, while still making physical contact with me, she turns her head around and gives me a glazed, slutty smile. Yes, there had been one too many before dinner drinks. She was very drunk. Fortunately, the buffet line began to move and I was sure to maintain an assured clear distance from then on. She said nothing about this incident the following Monday and I never brought it up, I mean I never mentioned it again.

But women do realize that they can get away with more in the office than the guys when it comes to sexual harassment behavior. In one office where I worked, the women held a "best buns" contest. They made up ballots and voted for the guy with the best buns in the office. You know that if the guys had a similar contest for the ladies and got caught, there would be hell to pay.

Still the ladies kept their contest, very hush-hush. I was actually one of the first guys to learn about it very soon after the results were tabulated. That's because I received an award in the contest. I was voted "Most Personable Buns". As this news filtered out, I took much ridicule from my male co-workers for winning what amounted to the "Miss Congeniality" award. However, this didn't bother me in the least. If I received this recognition, it meant my buns were on the ballot; my buns were in the game. For two weeks, the ladies in the office were spending work time evaluating my butt. I was, therefore, proud of winning "Most Personable Buns" and walked around the office for the next few weeks with my head and my buttocks held high.

*Postview: After this post, everyone asked me if the story about the woman sitting on the desk was true. The expression on my face before I said a word, told the answer. Seriously, I could not make this up. The next question from all the guys: Was she hot? The answer is "yes". Unfortunately that led to more questions, which eventually led me to repeat a famous Bill Clinton quote: "I did not have sexual relations with that woman." But unlike Bill, I am telling the truth.*

## What Not To Wear: Office Version

*Preview: I kept seeing articles on the business-networking site LinkedIn on how to dress for success and what was acceptable to wear under "business casual" rules. I decided to join the discussion, of course, from my warped perspective, and give examples of "what not to wear" at work. None of these stories are made up. They couldn't be; they are just too weird.*

> *They come runnin' just as fast as they can Coz' every girl's crazy 'bout a sharp dressed man.*
> *- ZZ Top*

Ever since my post dealing with men's fashion, I have been inundated with guys asking me the question: "How do I dress for success in the office?" Well, I have never been Mr. GQ, but I do have some examples on what not to wear in business situations.

## Not on the Golf Course, Not Anywhere

Years ago, Engineer Mike and I made an early morning sales call on a truck service dealer in Pennsylvania. We were wrapping up a very successful meeting when disaster almost struck. That's when Engineer Mike asked, "So you guys are going golfing?" He said this because one of the men was wearing one of the most hideous pairs of pants I have ever seen. They were plaid and the most dominant color, was yes, pink. But the guy looked at Mike and said very seriously, "No we're not going golfing." He obviously was confused and offended by the question and wanted an explanation why it was asked. The true answer was that the pants he was wearing should not ever have been made, should never have been sold, should never have been bought and obviously should never have been worn by him. Or "because your pants are hideous man".

I blurted out, "We'll it's such a beautiful morning, we just thought you might be golfing." Mike then quickly changed the subject and the sale was saved. We laughed about it for about five minutes in the car after leaving.

And by the way, the man rules (no pink below the belt) still apply even on the golf course. You can dress wild, you can dress crazy, but you can't dress pretty. Hey Alice! Unless you are planning to hit off the ladies tees, no pink below the belt.

## Plaid Is Bad

Pink plaid is wrong anywhere, but plaid is just plain bad in the office. A co-worker named Ezra had two pairs of plaid pants (one red, one green) that were a regular part of his office wardrobe. He looked absurd wearing the red and green plaid pants and took a great deal of ridicule from his co-workers. It is never a good thing when ladies are looking at your crotch area and laughing, especially when your pants are still on.

These type of plaid pants are only appropriate when you are smoking a pipe and drinking wine in your study at home (which I of course never have done). However, they are still not acceptable if they in any way decrease your chances of having sex later that day.

A man who wears plaid pants in the office; I know what you are thinking, but you are wrong. Ezra is Caucasian, very Caucasian. He would return from a Florida vacation whiter than before he left. Also, he is very heterosexual. I know this because he would frequent strip clubs and then brag about it. I never got to ask him if he ever wore his plaid pants to the club. I can't imagine that the strippers would enjoy performing a plaid lap dance. Of course, if the stripper was wearing a plaid skirt it would give a whole new meaning to "scotch doubles".

## Solids Aren't "Safe" Either

One day Intern Steve decided to wear his orange pants to the office. You are probably thinking they were a dark, burnt orange, but you would be wrong. He looked like a freakin' walking traffic cone. It is the only time I have laughed out loud at someone's pants. Again, it should be illegal to sell pants that outrageous, but Intern Steve made the decision to buy these things and to wear them to work. Understandably, Intern Steve did not get a job offer, allowing him to take his talents and his orange pants to another company. (The Geekyhood of the Traveling Orange Pants)

## No Yakking

Intern Earl decided to wear a very unique, brown furry jacket to the company Christmas party. When asked about his jacket, Earl proudly proclaimed that his jacket was made from "pubic hair from yaks" (I am not making this up). I didn't really believe him. I reasoned that you might be able to shave a yak in that area once and get away with it. The next time you touch him there, I think he bites your hand off. Still, I made sure that I went through the buffet line before Earl just in case his jacket shedded in the beef stroganoff. Not long after that incident, Earl and his amazing, yakky, hairy, scream coat were sent packing.

## But She's Not Chinese

I can't finish this post about men's clothes without mentioning Trisha the HR representative. She was kind of a "plain Jane", but she caused quite a stir in the office because she wore men's  shoes. I swear you could find her footwear on page four of the Thom McCann catalogue or maybe page one of the Butch McCann version. The women in the office hated her shoes. It was very disconcerting for them to be in the restroom and look down and see a pair of "man shoes" in the next stall. That's just too creepy. In a Hitchcock movie, the man shoes would have grown eyes to stare at the squatting victim. Trisha's office nickname was "manshoes", and therefore her tenure at the company was known as The Manshoe Dynasty.

> Pink Shirt, Plaid Pants
> But I can't get anyone to even dance
> Yak Suit, Odd Shoes
> I am dressed to really lose
> They go runnin' just as fast as they can
> Coz' no girl's crazy 'bout a dork dressed man.

*Postview: This turned out to be a popular post since most office workers can relate to seeing fashion faux pas in the workplace.*

# I'm Conducting Business Like A CEO – (Working From Home - Part 1)

*Preview: It was quite an adjustment to go from working in an office for 30 years to working at home. This adjustment was so involved it provided material for two posts. And yes, some of the material here was enhanced for comic effect.*

After spending my entire business career in an office environment, I recently changed jobs and became a "tele-commuter". Of course this is a misnomer, because in the digital age you can work from home and spend very little time actually on the telephone.

This obviously was a big change, and I was worried about being "unconnected" and isolated. Well, I am definitely not unconnected; in fact I am over connected. I have my own "command center". I can now receive calls on three phones (business, home and cell), do FaceTime, and receive e-mails on two accounts. I fear the day when all three phones ring, I get "FaceTimed" and important e-mails arrive all at the same time. I think trying to decide which one to answer first would throw me into "digital shock" which I doubt is covered by Obamacare.

The challenge is to make your home office seem as much like a real office as possible. You need to do this so that you never realize you are actually at home and not at "work". If that ever happens, you will end up on the couch in your pajamas, eating Cheetos and watching ESPN all day.

There are major benefits to working at home. I now have a ten-step commute from the bedroom to the office chair. Now on some days this can take longer if the doors are closed or if there is stuff on the floor I have to walk around. In addition, it is great to have a private bathroom at work. At three previous employers, the CEO had a private bathroom off their office. One time during a meeting, I actually got to take a whizz in the executive toilet. It is one of the highlights of my business career! (If only I would have been able to take a dump there, but I can only dream) And now I have an executive bathroom of my own where I can conduct my business in executive comfort, just like a CEO! At my old job, my co-workers always complained about that "guy" who always stunk up the bathroom. Well, now I think they were full of it. My bathroom at home smells just like the bathroom did at work, so I think that's just how bathrooms are supposed to smell.

People think you can become dull and boring if you work at home, but nothing is further from the truth. In fact, I have become much smarter since I changed jobs. As soon as I started working from home, my fantasy football team was virtually unbeatable. I won the league, and this was my first year of playing fantasy football ever! Yes, I am pretty smart. It was finding that rookie seventh-round draft-pick out of the Mississippi School for the Blind that won me the title (and the cash).

I am also much more popular since I started working at home. My number of Facebook friends has doubled. This includes Maya the young Filipino stripper who is trying to raise enough money to come to America to marry a wealthy businessman. And Maya thinks I'm cute! Hooyah!

Sometimes it is difficult to simulate a normal office environment. For example, it is difficult to have "casual" Fridays when you are working in "sweats" all week. I solved that problem by instituting "Pant-less Fridays". This was going swimmingly until the female UPS driver showed up one Friday with a delivery. Now it could have been worse, only a few of the neighbors heard the scream and nobody called the police. Let's just say I was happier to see her package than she was to see mine.

And then on another Friday, I was "Face Timing" with our administrative assistant (who lives in Florida) when I had to stand up to reach some files. You know I really have a problem with Apple calling something "Face Time" when in reality people can see more than just your face. I mean, who knew? That is just plain wrong. I am just glad sexual harassment laws do not extend across state lines.

So I replaced "Pant-less Fridays" with "Underwear Optional Fridays" which allows me to go commando in my command center. I just love making important business decisions free from being constrained by my underwear. On a related note, my boss has instructed me to make no important decisions of Friday's without checking with him first.

*Postview: This post was more popular with people who work from home because they can relate to my situation. I still encounter people who can't understand how I can function as a remote employee. I was able to make certain jokes in this post because I now work for a small company, versus a bastard corporation, and my boss does have a sense of humor.*

## Taking Care of Business (Working From Home – Part 2)

*Preview: I never thought that the most challenging thing about working at home would be managing my dog.*

The worst thing about working at home is the isolation. You are doing work, but you are alone all day. However, I am not truly alone. I am assisted in my important corporate tasks by my miniature German schnauzer, Midnight.

The problem is Midnight never attended business school and thus lacks the business acumen necessary to be a good assistant. He assumes the reason that I am now at home is to attend to his demands, not the company's, and it is very different having a dog as a coworker.

Midnight sometimes smells and is very irritating. Okay, so maybe I have had some coworkers over the years like that. Midnight occasionally makes disgusting noises. Yes, once again I have heard those in the workplace. And Midnight scratches himself in inappropriate places. Oh yeah, there was this guy who used to look at women during meetings and scratch his inner thigh with his middle finger. Midnight is not nearly as obnoxious and irritating as that guy.

So maybe Midnight is more like a typical workmate than I thought. And it does relieve some stress when he wants his head scratched during the day. Yes, you can pet your dog, but you can't pet your coworkers. Well actually you can pet your coworkers. However, if you get caught doing this with the administrative assistant in the back of the supply room, apparently the HR department gets very upset. And if your HR manager is a fat, old, ugly battleax, she is not going to understand your explanation and is going to put the incident on your "permanent record" which I'm sure is now in the possession of the government or even the Chinese.

Midnight does have a workstation in my office, which consists of a pillow and blanket so he can sleep while I do all the work. If I try to keep him out of my office by closing the door, he gets very offended just like my old butthead boss Steve. If I closed my office door, Steve would always find some stupid reason to barge in, even one time when I was having a very personal discussion on my lunch break. And no, this discussion was not with the administrative assistant mentioned earlier. We held all our important "discussions" in the supply room.

Midnight has mastered one business technique: the ability to sleep through long, boring, conference calls. We are all talking and yakking away and Midnight just enjoys a very deep sleep. But sometimes the sleep is even too deep.

> Boss   (during conference call): Ake, is that you snoring?
>
> Me:     No sir, that was the dog. I mean yes the meeting is boring, but it's not that boring, I mean ....

Having the dog in the room during conference calls raises other issues as well:

> Boss:   (during conference call): Ake, did you just fart?
>
> Me:     No sir, that was the dog.
>
> Boss:   But didn't you say you had Mexican for lunch?
>
> Me:     Yes sir, but it was the dog. I swear it was the dog.

Midnight:    Hell no it wasn't me. It was the double-bean burrito talking.

The most challenging aspect of having a dog as your work assistant is when he informs you five minutes before an important customer phone call that he has some business to conduct outside. Midnight does not care about the call because he has a more "pressing" deadline to meet. If I do not choose to take care of Midnight's business first, there can be dire consequences. Many times I have had coworkers figuratively crap on my project (Val the Bitch was great for this), but I have never had one literally do this.

So I leash Midnight and run out the door hoping that it is a quick trip. Midnight, however, has other plans. Just like I check for important e-mails, Midnight must check the yard for important p-mails. Of course these p-mails all say the same thing.

"Midnight, I stopped by. Didn't see you, so I peed in your yard". - Rover

In response, Midnight replies: "Rover, smelled that you had been here. Sorry I missed you, so I peed in the yard."

We think social networking is new. Dogs have been using the program "pisser" for eons.

So, my dog really does know how to take care of business. I may have an M.B.A. but Midnight graduated from the esteemed Bachman-Turner School of Business. It's the work that he avoids cause the dog's self-employed. He loves to work at nothing all day.

*Postview: After now working at home for 18 months, I have determined that Midnight is the best coworker I have ever had. I do love working at home. I do not think I could ever return to an*

*office/cubicle environment again. I'm sure I would try to strangle a coworker at some point.*

## Don's Excellent (Business) Adventure

*Preview: Some people love business travel; new places, new people, new experiences. I do not. I worry about things going wrong and my reaction to the unexpected, bad situations. This particular trip tested me almost from start to finish.*

It is best when business trips are uneventful. Of course, you want the "business" part to be successful, but you want the "trip" part to be boring.

Unfortunately, my recent trip to a trade show in Louisville was not boring. It was "eventful". The events of which I will journal here:

### Day 1

- The trip gets off to a fine start when my flight to Louisville is delayed due to a major mechanical problem, which took over an hour to repair. Normally, this would not be a big deal, but the delay caused me to miss my boss's big presentation. This was not good. Later in the day when potential customers asked me questions about the presentation, I responded with: "Hey, how about the weather in Louisville this year?"

- Fortunately, there were free appetizers provided after the conference, and I did get a free notepad and pen, so it wasn't a total waste.

- Then it was off to dinner with some potential customers. The plan here is to stuff these people so full of expensive steak that they buy something. Someone should make a video game out of it. You stuff steaks in the guy's mouth until he opens his wallet. Stuff too many steaks in there, however, and he pukes all over you.

- While walking downtown to the restaurant, I noticed a chunky-chicky wearing a micro-mini. Usually when you say a woman is showing off some leg, you are talking length. But in this case, it was length and width! And the wind was blowing - hey hey. I thought my 22-ounce rib eye would be the beefiest thing I saw that evening – but I was wrong.

- Fortunately, there were free appetizers before the meal. Actually, they weren't really free; they were very, very expensive. But they were free for me since I wasn't paying the bill. So hell yeah, I do want the last shrimp, thank you.

- The dinner experience was topped off by our flamboyant waiter Antonio, enthusiastically reading off the desert menu, and everything was "lusciously drizzled" in something!

## Day 2

- The day starts off by realizing I packed the wrong clothes for the trip. How I could possibly do this? I have no idea. Sometimes I can make a moron look intelligent. Which is ironic because .....

- I am considered an intelligent industry expert, and some investment people actually pay me to have breakfast with them. They ask me questions, I say expert type things, and they vigorously type the information into their tablets. I fail to mention that I cannot even manage to pack the correct clothes for a trip, and fortunately they do not ask why I am wearing flannel at this meeting.

- Then it is time for the actual trade show. My company doesn't have a display booth. I am there to make as many connections and trade as many business cards as I can. I end up walking almost seven miles and destroying a pair of socks in the process.

- That evening, I attend a reception where, fortunately, there are a plethora of free appetizers.

- I am at a table with a group of guys laughing, drinking and having a good time, when a game of "One-Up" begins. "One-Up is an unofficial, informal, game men play. It starts when one guy brags about something and then the other guys take turns "topping" the feat until someone says something that can't be topped and he is declared the "winner".

So, some guy casually mentions that his wife only weighs 110 pounds. The next "contestant" jumps in and says: "That's nothing, my wife weighs 105 pounds"

At this point, I decline to participate in the game. I do not know what my wife weighs. I could ask, but I still would not know, and it would be the last question I would ever ask in this life. This subject is on a strictly "need to know" basis, and trust me, I do not need to know.

I do not want people snickering at my funeral. "Why did she kill him?" someone would inquire. "I heard he asked her how much" ...... massive snickering...... I think it is a statistical probability that my wife weighed 105 pounds sometime in her life; however, I am not even going to speculate when that was. Let's just forget I even mentioned this.

After leaving that reception, I notice another reception across the hall. There is no one screening people at the door, so I enter and, fortunately, locate the free appetizers.

- I take a taxi back to the hotel. I tell my driver, Efanlinos (close to his real name), the name of my hotel and the street it is on. He drops me off and I head to my room, exhausted after a very strenuous day and my belly full of free appetizers. I go to elevator and notice something confusing. My room is on the fourth floor, but this hotel only has three floors. I was at the wrong hotel.

I will not explain how this happened, but I am not as stupid as you may think I am right now. Regardless, please don't mention this incident to the people who paid to eat  breakfast with me. I call Efanlinos (he was picking me up in the morning); he returns and attempts to blame me for the mix up. No Efanlinos, I gave you the correct hotel and THE STREET, you $%#*ed it up! You only missed it by nine miles!

## Day 3

- There is a young, hot female TSA agent barking out orders in the airport security line. I'm sort of enjoying it as she orders me to take off my jacket, shoes and belt. At my age, having a young, hot chick urgently demand that I remove my clothing is rather stimulating. I so much want to ask her "what she has in mind?" However, I know if I do, she will take me into a room and will penetrate me to the maximum with her wand. And I think she would really enjoy that, which means a twist is even possible. Because I will need to be seated for my two return flights, I decide to keep my mouth shut.

- The flights home are uneventful and I get on the airport shuttle to get to my car. Seated next to me is a very attractive South American woman talking loudly on her cell phone. I try not to follow the conversation (which was just stupid stuff), but it is almost impossible not to hear what she is saying under the circumstances.

  But when the driver pulls up to her car, she ends the conversation by saying in a hushed, sexy voice: "Bubble bath selfies, bubble bath selfies, bubble bath selfies!" and then jumps into her Mercedes.

  Bubble bath selfies, indeed .....

  What a trip.

*Postview: This actually overall was a positive experience for me. Even though a myriad of things went wrong, I maintained my composure and business-wise the trip was deemed a success! And there were free appetizers.*

📖 📖 📖

# CHAPTER 9

# Thoughts On Being A Man

I TRY TO REPRESENT MEN AS THEY ARE, NOT AS THEY SHOULD be. I'm not saying it's good. I'm not saying it's right. I'm just saying this is reality. Men are not that complex, not nearly as complex as women. The mistake women make is although they can understand men, they don't like what they discover and, thus, set out to change things.

Most men also happen to be at least somewhat insecure in their masculinity. We are often unsure and clueless. So I am also providing a needed service by informing men what behaviors are acceptable and which are not.

## Man Rules For Wearing Pink

*Preview: I have worn pink shirts and ties for a long time. I had received some criticism from guys for doing so, so I came up with my rules when men could wear pink. I knew I had something useful when I encountered a guy at work who said sarcastically:*

*"That's a pretty pink shirt (it was actually rose) you've got there."
Without hesitation, I read him "the rules". He stood there speech-
less as I walked away.*

I needed to buy some new casual shirts but I was perplexed to learn that all of the fashionable ones were called
"polo" shirts. I wasn't planning to play any polo, why did I
need a polo shirt?

Polo has to be one of the lamest sports of all time. The
horse does all the grunt work. All the player does is swing a
mallet violently at a small ball. It is dangerous, too. You can
fall off the horse at a high rate of speed, get whacked by a
mallet, or get hit by the ball.

So why was polo a popular activity? Because it was so
exclusionary. For example:

"May I play in the polo match today sir?

"While sure you can young peasant. Just go get your
horse."

"Why I don't have a horse, sir."

"Well, I guess you won't be playing then. But I have a
splendid idea about how you can participate. Here's a shiny
shovel. When we stop to partake of refreshments, you may
go clean the field for us."

But polo did give us the polo shirt.

One day Reginald arrived for the match wearing a peculiar garment.

"Reginald what is that shirt you are wearing?"

"I did not want to get my fine linen shirt soiled during
the match so I had my seamstress make me this shirt to wear
while playing polo. I have no idea what I will call it."

So the "polo" shirt was born. It was much later that commoners like me could have the thrill of wearing an actual polo shirt without having enough coin to actually play polo.

Therefore, it was determined polo shirts are what I wanted, and I started to search the sales flyers for possible purchases. I was surprised to see a pink polo shirt advertised for men. I have worn pink dress shirts for a long time.

Some co-workers have questioned this choice and because of this I have developed a rule about men wearing pink: "Men can wear pink clothing above the belt." Pink dress shirts and ties, yes. Pink belts, pants, socks and shoes, no.

Of course, this leads to the question: "What about pink underwear?" Obviously this is never permissible, even if your girlfriend wants you to. But this part of the rule is still in effect even if a pair of your whities gets misplaced in the laundry and comes out pink. The contaminated shorts need to be discarded immediately. You should not wear them ever again. Your "boys" deserve better than that.

So I have lived by this rule for a long time, but now I was confronted for the first time by a pink polo. The problem is that a dress shirt is inherently male clothing, but a polo shirt is not. It goes in the category of "ambidextrous" clothing that is bi-genderous.

After careful consideration, I concluded that my rule was still in effect. As a man, I could wear that polo and also not ridicule guys who did. However, I decided I would not buy that particular shirt due to "fashion" factors.

Everything was fine until the next Sunday when I perused the sales flyers after a big meatloaf dinner. There was another pink polo advertised, but this one had white horizontal stripes.

And it was probably the meatloaf talking, but as I stared at the flyer I thought:

> And I would wear any polo shirt
> I'd run right into Kohl's and back
> I would wear any polo shirt
> I wouldn't flinch and that's a fact
>
> But I'll never accept how those stripes look right
>    now, oh no, no way.
> And I would wear any polo shirt
> Oh I would wear any polo shirt
> I would wear any polo shirt
> But I won't wear that
> No I won't wear that.

Therefore, I have amended my rule that pink shirts are still permitted provided they don't have white stripes. Guys should also be careful of wearing pastel polo shirts that have white stripes.

## Some Closing Thoughts on Polo

Incredibly the game of polo is still being played today and it is still exclusionary. There are not polo teams or polo leagues, but polo clubs. Don't have enough money to join the club? No polo for you, peasant boy. But I think that anyone still playing polo today is a bigger loser than Chris Bosh! (Hey, I can't dis that other Miami Heat player because he was born in Akron as I was, so that makes him my geographical homie). Note: The Miami Heat had just lost the 2011 NBA finals.

I would make serious improvements in the game of polo. First, I would get rid of the horses. Have the players run around the field to make it safer and improve the cardio workout. Then I would get rid of the mallets since players would get hurt if they whacked on the ankles or other sensitive parts. Maybe the players could just kick the ball. But the ball is too small and hard to be kicked around. So I will make the ball much larger and softer (inflatable perhaps). Hey, I think I'm on to something. I'm going to write some more rules and I'll let you know when I finish. In the meantime, any suggestions for a name of this new sport would be greatly appreciated.

*Postview: Guys absolutely loved this post. Not because they found it very humorous, because it was educational. It gave structure and guidelines on a subject that causes more apprehension than you might think. I almost considered starting an advice blog where men send in questions about acceptable male behavior.*

## Our Freedom is Busting Out All Over

*Preview: This post like many was inspired by an obscure news item. The article is ridiculous on its own, but of course I can put my own unique perspective on it. There are not many people who can write an entire, objective piece on fake breasts without offending anyone—okay, I probably offended someone.*

It is always inspirational when someone aspires to achieve greatness. So we should all be lifted up by the story of Paula Simonds who wants to have the greatest (read largest) breasts in the world. (According to a report by the dailymail.com).

Most people who strive to attain greatness must train, strain and work very hard to achieve their goal. But Paula (stage name Lacey Wildd) will not need to do any of that (you knew she wouldn't be jumping rope or doing jumping jacks). No, to live her dream, Paula will have to undergo her 13th augmentation surgery to pump up her L-cup breasts to Triple-M (gives a whole new meaning to the term "Mmm, Mmm, good!").

This raises the question: Can you have too much of a good thing? Personally, I do not prefer fake breasts, because they are in fact, fake. It is akin to bra stuffing. It doesn't matter to me if the falsies are on the outside or the inside; they are still "false". It doesn't matter if your "date" is 5% plastic or 100% plastic (as in blow-up doll). Plastic is still plastic. Implants are acceptable for medical reasons or if a woman is a member of the IBTC (Itty, Bitty, Titty Committee). But if you are adequate, I see no reason to become more than adequate.

Of course, I know this opinion is in the minority among guys. Most guys love big, firm, fake breasts. But can men be so clueless and dense to be fooled by bags of silicone strategically placed? Okay, stupid question. Put a pair of large, fake hooters in front of a man and his brain completely shuts down. Got fooled for the hundredth straight time!

Yes, most men are obsessed with women's breasts whether they are real or not. And the bigger the breasts, the bigger the obsession. A few years ago, a woman was hired at a company and the guys who worked there suspected that her breasts were enhanced. For the next two weeks, a team of engineers worked diligently to determine the critical answer to this burning question. Using AutoCAD to simulate key waist-hip-bust ratios, they were able to come to a thrilling conclusion: Yes, they were fake, and yes, they were spectacular. The company soon learned to use this woman to walk around the office and collect the contributions for company charities because it is very difficult for a guy to say "no" to fake breasts. Contributions busted all previous totals!

But, I think it would be very difficult to be married to Paula (she is a divorced mother of five). Could you sleep soundly at night knowing that at any moment she could roll over and smother you to death? Sure, what a great way to go, but you would still be dead. In addition, you would constantly have to be careful about those jugs smacking you in the face. It would be embarrassing to go to work with black eyes and have your co-workers ask you if your wife beat you up again. Of course, you could always say, "No, I just got pummeled again by her humongous breasts. By the way, how was your evening?"

And lovemaking would be an adventure. First you would have to wear safety goggles because just like a Red  Ryder BB gun, those guns could put your eye out. Older guys would need something longer lasting than Viagra, because it would take more than an hour of foreplay to "adequately cover the terrain". And I think you would need extremely large hands, like an NFL wide receiver, to keep those things under control. If you have small hands and the session got too passionate, there could be structural damage to your house.

So even though I admire Paula's ambition, I cannot endorse this. Her children are against this due to the danger of "stretching, tearing and rupture", and this is just what could happen to the clothesline when she hangs her bras out to dry. Even though I do not agree with Paula, this is America. So as we celebrate Independence Day, let's be grateful that we live in a country where women have the freedom to enhance (and over-enhance) if they want to. This is a great country!

*Postview: I realized fake breasts were debatable issue when my three friends and I had a discussion on the topic and I was the only one who preferred "natural". This post also gives men the freedom to choose! What a great country indeed! Paula did not have the 13th surgery, but made the news again in 2014 when she had plastic surgery on other parts of her body.*

## The Most Middle-Aged Man In The World

*Preview: Becoming middle-aged is challenging for a man, but it also provides some amusement. This August 2011 post is a spoof of "The Most Interesting Man In the World" commercials from Dos Equis beer.*

He used to smoke joints, now his joints are smoked.

He still listens to K.C. & The Sunshine Band . . . on an 8-track player.

He has more hair growing on his back, than is growing on his head.

He is . . . the most middle-aged man in the world.

I don't eat ice cream often, but when I do, I prefer dos de cucharas (two scoops).

I don't dance often, but when I do, I prefer the dos paso (the two step).

I don't drive sports cars often, but when I do, I prefer dos puertas (two doors).

He can explain the benefits of a Roth IRA.

He smokes a pipe . . . filled will legal substances.

He has man-boobs that make teenage girls envious.

He is . . . the most middle-aged man in the world.

I don't drink Pepsi often, but when I do, I prefer dos litros (two liters).

I don't wear glasses often, but when I do, I prefer dos vidrios (two lenses).

I don't have threesomes often, but when I do, I prefer dos gemelas (two twins).

He knows why his wife is upset with him . . . without even asking.

He used to play lacrosse. Now he just drives one. (A Buick LaCrosse).

He believes corn-holing should be done only in private.

He is . . . the most middle-aged man in the world.

I don't wear footwear often, but when I do, I prefer dos zapatos (two shoes).

I don't fly small planes often, but when I do, I prefer dos motors (two engines).

I don't get complete physical exams often, but when I do, I prefer dos enfermeras (two nurses).

He knows how to properly hit a lob wedge.

He used to go backpacking. Now he packs his back in ice.

He knows how much fiber he can eat . . . without blowing out his shorts (most of the time).

He is . . . the most middle-aged man in the world.

I don't eat hamburgers often, but when I do, I prefer dos pastelillos (two patties).

I don't shoot shotguns often, but when I do, I prefer dos canons (two barrels).

I don't marry trophy wives often, but when I do, I prefer veintidós años de edad (22-year olds).

He has experienced the benefits of compound interest.

The kids in the neighborhood call him the Buddha . . . but not for his wisdom.

He used to spend money to be authentically hip. He now spends it on artificial hips.

He is . . . the most middle-aged man in the world.

I don't tee off often, but when I do, I prefer dos maderas (two woods).

I don't play poker often, but when I do, I prefer dos ases (two aces).

I don't use small bills often, but when I do, I prefer dos dolares (two dollars).

He can calculate his own cholesterol level.

He knows the best way to prepare for a colonoscopy.

He just bought a new shaver . . . for his ear hair.

He is . . . the most middle-aged man in the world.

I don't use sugar often, but when I do, I prefer dos cubos (two cubes).

I don't throw fastballs often, but when I do, I prefer dos costuras (two seamers).

I don't wear bras often, but when I do, I prefer dos copas (two cups).

Keep breathing my friends ......

*Postview: I really like this one. I think it is humorous and creative, but the response was not as great as expected. I guess this man is not as interesting as I imagined .....*

## Preventing Female Riots And Sex Strikes

*Preview: Pussy Riot is actually a Russian, feminist, punk-rock group. In 2012 they were arrested for singing protest songs, and their plight made the U.S. news. This resulted in news reporters everywhere having to say the phrase "Pussy Riot" without cracking up on the air. I wondered what would happen if there were actual a literal pussy riot. What would be the consequences for men throughout the world?*

Men around the world should be concerned about the alarming events occurring in Russia. Some very upset women have organized something called a "Pussy Riot". I don't know exactly why they are rioting, but they have stood up to threats by Russian President Vladimir Putin. Now Putin is one tough Ruskie, but these chicks are putting it to Putin.

But, this Pussy Riot is a serious threat to men everywhere. These Pussy Rioters are enflamed. Something has stroked the passion deep within them. I know that in most cases this would be a good thing, but in this case it is a bad thing, a very bad thing.

I am very concerned that the Pussy Riots could spread to this country just as the "Arab Spring" protests spread to numerous places last year. Once a few Pussy Rioters get upset, they could start whining to their friends on Facebook and this movement could go worldwide. Remember, it used to be that when you did something stupid and upset your wife, the only other women that got upset were her co-workers and the friends that she called. Now, because of the "social media", you can actually goof up and fizz off women throughout the world!

But we must take extraordinary measures to head off this Pussy Riot before it starts in America. Therefore, I am imploring men everywhere to enact the following measures immediately and to continue this behavior until this most serious threat has passed.

> 1. Return the toilet seat to its downward and sitting position.

This includes after trips in the middle of the night and after rushed trips during commercial breaks in football games.

> 2. Actually make an attempt to listen to your wife or significant other (WOSO) when she speaks to you.

I know this may be burdensome, but you just have to focus. If she starts to share one of the problems that her friend is having during the fourth quarter of an important NFL game, just pretend to listen while still focusing on the game. This is the relational equivalent of Peyton Manning looking-off the safety while really watching the receiver on the other side of the field.

3. Spend more time on foreplay.

If you don't know what foreplay is, I suggest that you Google it. If you need some new ideas, Google is good for that also. Just don't get caught looking at the instructional videos or you will cause a Pussy Riot in your own house.

4. Extend the duration of the "act" itself.

I realize this combined with #3 is going to eat into the time you spend on your fantasy football league. But, unless you are involved in one of those "high stakes" leagues, stopping a raging Pussy Riot is worth the effort.

I have read that humming "Twinkle, Twinkle, Little Star" is a good way to make sure that you spend enough time on the task. Just remember not to hum out loud. Other guys say they think about Rosie O'Donnell if they find things progressing too fast. This may be too extreme for some men however.

5. Be nice to your mother-in-law.

I have confidence you can do this if you really try. Just remember that your mother-in-law will be one of the Pussy Rioters if it comes to your city and you really, really do not want that.

6. Pick up your socks and underwear and place them in the hamper.

It will be herculean efforts like this that will keep the Pussy Riots contained. In this case your WOSO is correct. This stuff is really not going to pick itself up.

7. Make your own damn sammich!

If you've forgotten how, you need to use Google once again.

8. Take your WOSO out to dinner.

This must be at a restaurant that does not use plastic utensils. Always do this the day before a big football game. Hopefully, your WOSO will talk so much at dinner that she will not then cause unfortunate interruptions during the game.

9. After dinner, take her to the movie of her choice.

Of course, this will be a chick flick, and it will probably have an emotional ending that will cause her to cry. All you have to do is to wait to the end of the movie and think about how bad your fantasy football team is going to do because you just wasted two hours in the theatre instead of making those great trades. This should bring tears to your eyes at just the appropriate time.

10. Buy her some flowers.

When you go to pick up beer for the game, just buy one of those cheap bouquets they have at the store. If you don't have enough cash, unfortunately you will have to buy a cheaper brand of beer. Penn State fans are exempt from this one since they are going to need to drink hard liquor to make it through this season.

I know these actions may seem severe and extreme, but the prospect of Pussy Rioters marching down your street is just too harrowing. So men, we can get through this if we just stick together and keep our potential Pussy Rioters satisfied.

*Postview: The real Pussy Riot eventually got out of jail. Someone reading this post somewhere did feel the need to write and inform me that I was confused and Pussy Riot was actually the name of a band. Really? I love it when that happens.*

## These Women Are Turning Me Fifty Shades of Red

*Preview: Fifty Shades of Grey is a cultural phenomenon; this is my warped spin on it.*

You would think by now I would be an expert in communicating with women, but recently I have had several strange conversations that ended with ladies becoming upset and disappointed. For example:

- I called my insurance agent Tina because she had made several errors on a recent quote.

    "I'm very sorry about the mistakes I made", she said. "I've been a very bad agent. Would you like to spank me?"

    "Now, now, everyone makes mistakes," I said. "Just send me a corrected quote and we'll be good."

"Fine", she said curtly. "I just send you a new quote then."

- I was at my doctor's office getting my blood pressure checked when the nurse said: "I really enjoyed cuffing you. I think it would be great if you cuffed me. I'm sure it would raise your blood pressure."

  Of course I declined the offer. She's the medical professional. I don't see any benefit of me taking her blood pressure! And, shouldn't she be trying to lower my blood pressure?

- I told a vendor that I couldn't meet with her on Tuesday because I was tied up in a meeting.

  "Ooh, I just loved to be tied up", she said. "Would you like to meet some evening?"

  I told her that my schedule wasn't that tight and we could meet at my office Thursday morning. She seemed much less thrilled with this idea.

- At lunch one day I ordered the whipped potatoes. The waitress said:

  "I just love to get whipped. What do you think?"

  I told her that she should just get some potatoes to go when her shift was over and enjoy them at home.

- I was having this lunch with my friend Cherise, when we finished eating she said:

  "I want you to force me to do something I don't want to do."

  I thought quickly and replied, "Okay, you can pay for lunch. My food costs almost twice as much as yours, so I am really sticking it to you! And you're responsible for the tip also."

Cherise got real upset at the idea, so I guess she really didn't want to do this!

- My co-worker Gail said that she wanted to be disciplined and asked me if I wanted to help.

"Sure," I replied. "We all need more structure at the office. You can start by making a 'To Do' list every morning."

- I was returning books at the library when the librarian said:

"Would you like it if I got very kinky?"

"Your hair looks very nice straight, but if you wanted to make it curly, give it a try," I said.

- The perky clerk at Starbucks took my order and then asked:

"I want to get into S&M. Can you help me?"

I told her that sales and marketing would be a good field for her to consider and that I would let her know if I heard of any openings. She looked very disappointed at my reply.

I told my friend Roger about all these weird conversations, and he said that it all has to do with something called Fifty Shades of Grey. Now, this is just about the most ridiculous thing I have ever heard of. When I worked at a paint store, we had over 50 shades of off-white because people were very particular about getting just the right one to match their décor. But grey? All you really need are three shades of grey: light, medium or dark. One of those usually does the trick.

So ladies, if you are stimulated by the thought of fifty shades of grey, just go to your local paint store and tell the guy there what you really need. Be sure to be very explicit in your description because some guys are so dense they don't understand what a woman is really telling them. I'm sure the man at the paint store will be happy to satisfy any special desire you may have.

*Postview: Men do not know quite how to respond when a woman proclaims she has read this book – and that includes me. So I'll just stop here – okay?*

# CHAPTER 10

# Politics Can Be Humorous Too

I HAVE READERS WHO ARE FAR LEFT, I HAVE READERS WHO are far right, and I have readers who are so apolitical. Therefore, the blog tries not to take political stands. That being said, politics is a big influence in our culture and sometimes it creates humorous topics. So this chapter makes fun of the process as much as anything else. If you are right, left or just plain wacko, you will find something to laugh at in this chapter.

## My Big Presidential Endorsement

*Preview: This was posted right before the 2012 election. Two things to remember before reading: Both candidates choose Catholics as running mates and both candidates had grandfathers who were in polygamous relationships.*

I thought it would be a good idea to remind everyone the presidential election in just two weeks away, just in case you have been living under a rock the past few months. Of course, there is no need to remind anyone here in Ohio, since it is considered a "swing" state. This does not mean that we are frequently engaging in kinky sex. No, it means that we have not decided yet who we will vote for. Of course, it is difficult to concentrate on politics when you are having so much kinky sex.

This campaign has been rather contentious. It has divided families. It has divided co-workers. And in the most serious rift, it has divided Facebook friends. It's just like the Civil War except for all the dead bodies and that secession thing. People are posting stupid, inane, bigoted and outright ridiculous things on Facebook, and these are just from the candidates. My Facebook friends are posting much worse.

In order to end the war between my Facebook friends, help my Filipino Facebook friends decide who to vote for, and most importantly, to stop the constant political phone calls and the pile of daily political mailings, I have decided to make my much-anticipated presidential endorsement.

## My Choice

My Guy has the correct position on all of the issues. And even when he is proven wrong on an issue, he backtracks with grace and dignity and quickly develops new positions, which are even more excellent than the previous ones. However, Your Guy is an unprincipled, flip-flopper who is very shady. My Guy is always totally honest on all things. Your Guy is a bold-faced liar who can't be trusted on anything. My Guy waxes eloquently, while Your Guy has wax in his ears and can't even hear the voice of the people.

I have heard some very disturbing things about Your Guy's religious beliefs. I am concerned that he is some "wacko" nut job whose weird beliefs surely influence every decision that he makes. My Guy's religious beliefs are very mainstream and he is very close to sainthood.

My Guy's political ads clearly state the truth with no distortions and deceit whatsoever. However, Your Guy runs ads that are so silly they are laughable. Nothing in these ads is true, especially the outrageous lies about My Guy.

I think by now we know which candidate is the best master debater. Your Guy was rude, dishonest and disrespectful. My Guy acted with the upmost dignity and displayed an almost angelic demeanor. I do realize that both guys were too aggressive in the second debate, but I attribute that to them trying to impress that gorgeous hunk of woman, Candy Crowley, who is one part Victoria Secret model and one part Chicago Bears linebacker. Groooowl!

My Guy selected a Catholic running mate who is a living embodiment of God. However, I have heard priests criticize Your Guy's Catholic running mate as being a sinner and no better than a Baptist! Your Guy's grandfather had multiple wives in a foreign country and My Guy's grandfather, uh, okay let's forget that one.

I fully believe all the polls that show My Guy winning the election. These polls are done by outstanding research firms that utilize the best practices available. The polls that show Your Guy ahead are total rubbish. They use methods such as voodoo, Ouija boards and fortunetellers to get their numbers. And these polls totally ignore My Guy's ability to inspire the electorate and make a stunning comeback.

So I believe the choice is obvious. For all these reasons, I am strongly endorsing "My Guy" for President of the United States. And may I add, Your Guy is a total doo-doo head.

May God bless My Guy and may God bless the United States of America!

*Postview: I won't say if My Guy won or not, but Your Guy is still a total doo-doo head. Somebody complained after reading this that they couldn't tell which candidate I was endorsing --- Mission accomplished!*

## Sometimes Democracy Stinks

*Preview: I don't know how I find myself in such awkward situations. It was a simple trip to the voting location, in an "off-year" election. This event is funny now, but it wasn't very funny then.*

These are the people at your polling place, at your polling place, at your polling place

These are the people at your polling place, the people that you meet Tuesday

Last November, I exercised my right as a United States citizen and voted. I admit that I was a bit cranky as I drove to a local church after work to cast my ballot. It was dark and rainy, and I was tired and hungry. More importantly, I knew the only issue I really cared about was going down in defeat. But I still wanted to vote so my side would end up losing by one fewer vote. And it worked! Due to my efforts, the issue only lost by 792,249 votes instead of 792,250 (actual count). So stick it other side, stick it really hard.

I wanted a quick, uneventful, voting experience, but that wasn't going to happen. As soon as I entered the hall, I encountered a most horrific smell. I soon realized the source of the stench was the 20-something dude standing directly in front of me. He will hereafter be referred to as "Young Stinky Guy". I don't know how long you have to go without bathing to create such body odor, but I actually looked to see if there was a toxic cloud hovering over his head. It should be illegal to smell this bad.

Young Stinky Guy was trying to decide where his precinct table was located. I knew mine was to the left, and I was  so hoping his was to the right, but of course he finally turned left. So I was stuck right behind him, inhaling his fumes, but fortunately the line was not too long.

However, then Clueless Unregistered Guy entered the picture. It took a while for those lively poll workers to determine that this person was not registered to vote. When informed of this, he smiled sheepishly and said, "Well I've been out of the country for a while, so maybe that's why."

No, you don't lose your citizenship if you leave the country, you moron. You are not registered because you didn't register. And now you decide to show up here at one of the busiest times of the day and expect to vote. So then Aged Poll Worker Guy has to find a provisional voting application and slowly and thoroughly explain to Clueless Unregistered Guy how to complete it. And all the while, I continue inhaling the remnants of Young Stinky Guy.

While we waited, I was tempted to offer some manly advice to Young Stinky Guy about the benefits of soap. He really could have used some (both the advice and the soap). I know he doesn't have a girlfriend unless the woman has no sense of smell or better yet has no nose at all. He probably doesn't have a job unless he works as a diver at the sewage treatment plant.

But just when I thought things couldn't get worse, Old Blind Guy gets in line behind me. I had noticed him in the parking lot as his daughter was helping him make it slowly to the door. I knew he was standing behind me because I was naturally trying to keep a large gap between me and Young Stinky Guy, but Old Blind Guy was violating the guy rule of assured clear distance and was bumping up next to me. Normally, I would have turned around and given him a dirty look, but that wasn't going to work now, was it? Saying "Is that your white cane or are you that excited about the candidates?" was not an option either.

However, this created an ethical dilemma. What is the protocol when standing in line in front of a blind person? Do I let him cut in front of me? What is the rule? I didn't have a clue, but it was making me very uncomfortable. I did feel compassion for him. I did feel sorry for him. However, there was one person in the room that I felt even sorrier for. That would be the person directly behind him in line. And then I had an epiphany. If I let Old Blind Guy cut in front of me, the person directly behind him in line would in fact be me. You may disagree with what I did, but no cutsies this time.

I finally got my access card, went to the voting machine (one next to Young Stinky Guy of course) and made my selections. In Ohio, we actually got to vote on the healthcare bill. I thought it was ironic that I was voting on this with vastly more knowledge of the subject than Congress had when they rushed to vote on it in 2009. Heck, even Old Blind Guy knows more about it, and he is of course, blind. Is this a great country or what?

I finished voting and sure enough Old Blind Guy had still not made it through the sign-in process, and the line had now stretched to the door. As I left the church, I realized that Young Stinky Guy was probably one of those commie-hippie-freaks and had no doubt cancelled out all of my votes. There is, of course, a 50% chance Old Blind Guy (if not assisted) had nullified my choices also.

Driving home, I was still feeling somewhat guilty about not letting Old Blind Guy cut ahead of me, when I had my second epiphany of the night. I remember reading that if someone loses one sense, their other senses are enhanced. That means that if Old Blind Guy had an enhanced sense of smell and I caused him to stand too close to Young Stinky Guy, he would now be dead. Therefore, I am not a cad; I am a democracy-loving hero.

*Postview: This post oddly enough caused a debate at work. People thought I should have let Old Blind Guy have cutsies. That is until I asked them what they would have done, then they quickly shut up and changed the subject.*

*Upon further review, Old Blind Guy's caretaker should have never taken him out after dark across an unpaved parking lot. Plus, it was not fair to the poll workers and people who had to wait an extended time behind him in line. That's why they have absentee ballots. So I do not feel any remorse now about my decision.*

## Billie Jean's Not My Problem

*Preview: Early in 2012, there was this huge debate about government-paid birth control pills. It was news every day, with congressional meetings and everybody debating the issue. Both sides spent money on advertising and robo-calls exhorting their views. I arrived home one day and found a very humorous message on my answering machine.*

Recently, I received a very disturbing phone call on my answering machine. It was from a very despondent, young woman who was almost to the point of tears apparently because I would not pay for her birth control pills.

This in turn was very alarming to me because in the words of Bill Clinton: "I did not have sexual relations with that woman." Whoops, bad example. But honestly, I am not stuffin' that muffin.

She sure was upset though, maybe she had the wrong number. Maybe she heard the rumors about me and Snooki and is trying to cash in. But I don't know her, never met her and we are not dating. I will henceforth refer to her as Billie Jean. Because Billy Jean's not my lover, she just a girl that claims that I owe her some.

Rest assured that if Billy Jean was my paramour, I would pay for her birth control pills. This is very rational. No married man wants to turn his chicky-babe into a chicky-mama. Oh no, I would buy the pills and not just cheap generics. It would be high-quality, name brand stuff. And it certainly wouldn't be the brand they sell at Wal-Mart with the Flintstones on the bottle. That brand has a photo of Wilma sporting a baby-bump with a circle-slash over it.

But as I said before, I am not involved in any dalliances with Billie Jean, Snooki or any other woman. Heck, I am not even sleeping with a Kardashian. I know that is difficult to believe and it puts me in the minority. I'm sure I could if I wanted, but I am just too busy to do it. I sure do hope that the Kardashians use high-quality contraceptives, because the last thing this world needs is more Kardashians.

Instead of calling me, I believe that Billie Jean should talk to her boyfriend and get him to pay for her pills. Guys who refuse to do this are stupid and irresponsible. It's just like at the amusement park where you have to buy a ticket to get on the ride. The ticket helps pay for a safe, pleasant experience without any unplanned consequences. They want you to stay happy even after you get off and go home.

Billie Jean told me that I should immediately call my congressman to help her get her contraceptives. I have no idea why. I really need to keep this thing on the down low and don't want to involve the government. I have heard that many politicians do have sex with younger women. Billie Jean, if you are having sex with the congressman, then by all means, he should be buying the pills. This is standard procedure. I'm sure Bill Clinton has paid for more birth control than a small free clinic. If you are calling to set up a threesome with the congressman, I am not into "that" as I think I made perfectly clear in a previous blog post.

She also suggested that I call Rush Limbaugh and complain to him. This is ridiculous. Under no means am I going to discuss this on the radio before millions of listeners. I am also not going to contact my bishop like she asked. I don't even have a bishop unless I am playing chess and I tend to lose those pieces first. I am not going to tell any clergyman that a young woman is upset with me because I won't buy her contraceptives, lest he think that Billie Jean is my lover.

So if you are reading this Billie Jean, please, please, no more phone calls. I do not want to explain to my wife why young women keep calling me about providing birth control pills for them. I don't want to dance, or moonwalk, around this anymore. And Snooki, please stop calling also. It's over; it's time to move on.

Billie Jean is not my lover

She's just a girl who claims that I owe her some

But the bill is not mine, son

*Postview: I can't even remember how this whole thing was resolved. Billie Jean never called back, so I am assuming she is happy now.*

## The Big Gulp is Evil!

*Preview: In May of 2012, New York Mayor Michael Bloomberg proposed a ban on the sale of large sodas and other sugary drinks in the city's restaurants, delis and movie theaters in an attempt to reduce obesity.*

The Mayor of New York City sure got everyone riled up with his proposed ban on large "sugary" drinks. The reaction has not been very sweet at all.

I think the issue is very confusing to most people. For example, I'm sure many older adults cannot understand why anyone would want to drink that much in one serving. And for anyone with "piping issues" regarding the bladder or the prostate, imbibing that much-carbonated beverage would seem ludicrous indeed. Why even the thought of downing that much soda pop would cause... uh oh eh, oh no. Please excuse me for one moment. I'll be right back..........

Ah, that is much better, yes. Where was I? Okay, people don't like the ban. But in the words of South Park Guidance Counselor Mr. Mackey: "Pop is bad, mkay. You shouldn't drink pop, because pop is bad, mkay."

And pop is bad. Studies have shown that the combination of high-fructose corn syrup and phosphoric acid will rot your innards (this is a medical term). And diet pop is supposed to be even worse for you, although scientists don't know why yet. This should scare the hell out of everyone, but it doesn't. The proposed ban doesn't even apply to diet soda, which may kill you faster.

Still, Americans don't like the government telling them what they cannot have. My socially conscientious friend Anne was outraged when she first heard about the proposed law. Even though she lives in Ohio, she had this ravenous, almost insatiable, craving to consume a Big Gulp. When her boyfriend heard about this, he immediately told her that the mayor of her town was thinking about banning sex between single people in her city. I don't know if Anne has calmed down any because I haven't heard from her (or her boyfriend) in days.

But do you really need that much soda? Back in my day, fifteen cents got you a bottle of Coke from the vending machine in my grandpa's grocery store. You didn't gulp it because it was only 6½ ounces and you needed to savor every sip. Sure we were still thirsty, but we could still fit into our britches and we didn't get diabetes as kids. No, my generation gets diabetes when we get older. And we get it by eating too much pie, which is the proper way. And encouraging people to gulp pop creates excess intestinal gas, which negatively impacts us all.

And there have been always fat kids. Growing up, I lived across the street from a kid my friend Fred referred to as "Whoa-Jelly"; his brother was called "Whoa-Jam". When this huge kid ran barefoot down the sidewalk, there was fat shaking everywhere, which always prompted Fred to yell out "Whoa-Jelly, Whoa-Jelly, Whoa-Jelly". The problem is that while Whoa-Jelly was an oddity then, he is everywhere now. We are becoming a Whoa-Jelly nation. Of course, in the past there were these people who actually put limits on what children ate, drank or did for their general welfare. These people were known as "parents". I'm not sure where these people went.

Nobody really needs that much soda pop at one time, but the government telling us how much to drink is too intrusive. I guess we can still consume, but in moderation.

However, the recent health studies tell us that maybe "moderation" should be way less than we current consume. Yes, we all need to be Buddhists on this one. Drinking a Big Gulp is not Zen-like in any fashion.

One shudders to think what could have happened in the Big Gulp existed in Buddha's day. I'm sure it got steamy sitting under that fig tree all the time, and you know that figs taste great with Pepsi. If one day Buddha got really hot and thirsty and said, "Forget this moderation stuff and bring me a Big Gulp now!," the world would have been deprived of a major religion.

*Postview: This proposal was battled in the courts until June 2014 when it was defeated. Drink up fat people!*

## No First Cougars Need Apply

*Preview: This post is from June 2011 as the 2012 race for President of the United States was just beginning.*

Recently, a prominent politician decided against running for President due to some past marital difficulties perpetuated by his wife. Initially, I was disappointed because I liked the guy and thought that past issues (happened in the 90s) should not matter.

However, on second thought, it is very important that our President has extreme marital stability. Our President has way too many other things to manage and worry about. His marriage needs to be stronger than Gibraltar and run smoother than silk.

This means the First Lady must be very stable and not promiscuous. We can have no desperate White-Housewives. I know what you are thinking: There have been no "hot" First Ladies since Jackie Kennedy (unless you count that vixen Barbara Bush). However, we live in a culture of second (and third) marriages and trophy wives. In the last campaign (2008), we had Jeri Thompson (Fred's wife) and Jill Biden (Joe's lady). This time, there is Callista Gingrich (Newt's latest squeeze). As a German guy once said, "Ya, Ya, Ya." So it is only a matter of time before there is a certified First Babe.

Now I know you want me to comment on the current First Lady. I will not go there. The only thing I will say is that women writers have commented on Michelle Obama's sexy arms. Okay, I have never, ever heard a guy comment on a woman's arms. On the list of interesting female body parts, arms fall somewhere below ankles and above chins. I know there is a video workout for women who want sexy arms, but ladies I'm telling you that is a waste of time and money. If arms are your best feature, then that says it all.

And of course, there is a double standard. Bill Clinton proved that you could tend to intern-al affairs and still run the country. You could even argue that Clinton's job performance was improved due to stress relief. In that case, Clinton may have been the least stressed President ever. Perhaps that's why he was smiling all the time. Come to think of it, he's still smiling. And he was also the most optimistic President. No matter how tough a day he had, it often had a happy ending.

But the First Lady has to act like, well, a lady first. Here are some basic rules of conduct that we should expect. No polishing any heads of state. No illicit introduction of members of Congress, and no exploring the Attorney General's briefs. She has to remain under control. This is extremely important because you don't want the following to happen:

(On the mobile radio)

Secret Service Agent One: "Raging Cougar is entwined with pool boy in the Lincoln Bedroom."

Secret Service Agent Two: "Confused. I recognize code name Cougar, but Pool Boy does not decode."

Secret Service Agent One: "Not Pool Boy, you idiot. The pool boy, she's banging the pool boy!"

Secret Service Agent Two: "Oh #!*$"

However I'm not sure a guy would be stupid enough to get involved with the wife of the most powerful man on earth.

Secret Service Supervisor: "What did you do with 'pool boy'?"

Secret Service Agent One: "We boarded him sir."

Secret Service Supervisor: "You water boarded him?!"

Secret Service Agent One: "No sir. Two-by-Four in the nuts. Pool boy won't be jumping back in that pool anytime soon."

And we can't have this, because when this happens, guys tend to hurt people and break things. We can't have the President get that enraged.

Newscaster: "Today, it was confirmed that the First Lady was caught 'entertaining' the White House pool boy in the Lincoln Bedroom."

"In a related story, the Afghanistan War ended abruptly today due to the fact that Afghanistan no longer exists. It is expected that the new hole in the ground will be renamed Af-gone-nistan."

So, it is a very important requirement that First Ladies remain pure. In addition, I would require that they are not permitted to nag or bitch at their husbands. The Congress bitches at the President. The commentators bitch at the President. Foreign leaders bitch at the President. That's too much bitching. So, the White House should be a "bitch-free" zone. Furthermore, the First Lady would not be permitted to complain about her husband to her friends, less the bitching get leaked to the press.

Now I know what you guys are thinking. The Republican race is wide open and four years of bitch-free living is very attractive (even some Democrats would be willing to run as Republicans to get that). But this is no reason to run for President, and it is a much more stressful job since the interns left.

*Postview: This was only the second ever "Ake's Pains". I received a scathing message from a woman who read this post and took it seriously. This was very affirming, it meant that I still had "it" and needed to use it!*

# CHAPTER 11

# The Wedding Chronicles

MY DAUGHTER CASSANDRA GOT MARRIED IN JULY OF 2014. I never really planned to "chronicle" this event, but so many things happened that I had to write about them. When I finished writing them all out, I had four blog posts and almost 4,000 words.

This chapter displays a more personal style of writing. This style change began early in 2014 in order to give more "life" to my writing and to better connect emotionally with my readers. It also meant that I had to express my feelings more, and thus become more vulnerable. These posts were very popular and I think people identified with many of the struggles I revealed.

The chapter also includes the only serious essay in the book: "Who'll Stop The Rain?" I didn't plan to include any serious posts in the book, but the "Wedding Chronicles" would not be complete without it.

## Father of the Bride
## (The Wedding Chronicles – Part 1)

*Preview: I realized how strange the role of "Father of the Bride" was almost from the beginning of the process. So I started developing this idea over a period of time and did plan to write this as a standalone, single post.*

From the moment you first hold your infant daughter, you take on a set of very important responsibilities of which you are totally unprepared for. Raising daughters is often like driving an old truck full of highly combustible materials down a very bumpy road. You can drive masterfully and still end up smoldering, holding what's left of the steering wheel.

The responsibilities get easier and less taxing once the teen years are over, but one major responsibility remains. It lurks out in the shadows, waiting to pounce when you least expect it. Then one day something called a "proposal" is made, and if accepted, this transforms you into an almost mystical being which our society labels "Father of the Bride" (FOB).

But this FOB thing is a really odd responsibility. And, when you are given a title that you did not seek, you can be sure you are being set up in some way. "Here's a nice, new, title. My aren't you special!" (Stupid sap you are!)" I was told to "save your money", but I was not told how much money to save or what it would be used for. In reality, nothing can prepare you for the financial beating you are about to receive.

As far as I can tell, the primary function of the FOB is to write frequent and sometimes enormous checks for everything and anything wedding related, checks that have many zeroes and commas. You are playing the role of the superhero "Father of the Bride", and bills and invoices come flying at you from all directions at warp speed. You must suppress these evil forces by all means necessary, using the super powers at your disposal; checks, credit cards, loans, whatever it takes!

The difficult part is that you are paying large amounts of money for things, which under normal circumstance you, would never, ever buy. Weddings would be so much different if men planned them, which is, of course, the reason men do not plan them. If they did, it would be a disaster.

However, weddings provide the opportunity for the women folk to go slightly insane doing extreme woman-type activities. The wedding planning is a series of estrogenically driven actions without any limits. It is estrogen unchained, it is estrogen unencumbered, it is estrogen overflowing! This results in things such as discussion and planning of every inch of the wedding dress. Women break down the details of the wedding dress similar to the way guys break down the details of a football game. The dress's train is discussed with the same enthusiasm and preciseness as a "Cover 2 Defense".

And this obsession with precise detail is repeated over and over again with the cake, the flowers, the attendants' clothing, the music, the table settings, the napkins, etc. The intensity of this effort reaches a crescendo the week of the wedding as the estrogen reaches dangerously high levels. It was so strong in my house I had trouble breathing. Now in some circumstances, high estrogen levels are a good thing (right guys?), but elevated amounts of estrogen always result in men paying some price. And this time, the price was enormous.

In the case of wedding planning, each attention to detail results in added expense, which the FOB is naturally expected to pay for. Fresh banana cake! Ba Ching! Top Deejay! Ba Ching! Special Flowers! Ba Ching. Etc., etc., etc., Ba Ching, Ba Ching, Ba Ching! That giant sucking sound was the money flowing out of my savings account.

And you have to pay it because it's your daughter's wedding, for heaven's sake! It's like a female version of the Mafia demanding extortion. It's a chance for payback against the male species and oh you are going to pay up big time.

I used to laugh when reading about FOBs who had to take out home equity loans to pay for a daughter's wedding. I thought the poor saps got suckered into paying for a very extravagant affair. I am no longer laughing. The average wedding today costs $30,000. Ours was a modest event and the cost of living here is low, so the total was much below that.

Now instead of laughing, I am crying. And it has nothing to do with the blessedness of the ceremony. I thought we were being prudent by serving chicken at the reception, but it was Chicken Cordon Bleu. I figure they had it flown in from France because the Chicken Cordon blew a hole in my bank account!

And just when I thought it was over, my wife asked me for a blank check on the day of the wedding to cover "extras". Extras? What could possibly exist that I hadn't paid for already? She said maybe this would be in case someone drinks too much. Drinks too much? I was raised a Baptist, in my view everyone is going to drink too much!

As I walked my daughter over the bridge to the gazebo where the vows were exchanged, I tossed 10 pennies out into the lake. The official story is that I did this to bring the couple good luck. In reality, it was the last 10 cents I had left, so I figured they might as well have that, too.

But I made it through, I did fulfill my obligation and, most importantly, none of the checks bounced! And I will be able to quit my new second job at the telemarketing firm as soon as I get my sales volume up. So if anyone needs some new aluminum siding for their house, please let me know.

*Postview: This may be the most complex piece I had ever written. Women enjoyed this post more than men because it was about a wedding. I had once again pointed out the difference between the sexes, without denigrating women. It was the most popular post in the Wedding Chronicles.*

*There was one group who did not find it very funny, former Fathers of the Bride. I think they found it affirming. The comments that I received said I had very accurately described the feelings of that situation, that I had captured the essence of the moment. If this is true, I think all future Fathers of the Bride need to read this one when the wedding date is set, so please share.*

## A Dysfunctional Dancing Machine (The Wedding Chronicles – Part 2)

*Preview: In order to write this one, I had to reveal a stupid decision and an utter failure. This was not easy for me to do; it was very uncomfortable and yet very funny.*

The Father of the Bride (FOB) has more responsibilities than just paying for the wedding. For me, the most daunting of these responsibilities was the father-daughter wedding dance. I have never been considered "light" on my size 13-feet.

My history of slow dancing is not impressive. My performance at my senior homecoming was so terrible that my date (who was very cute) never spoke to me again. My dancing at my senior prom was such that my date soon moved out of the country. The last time I slow danced was at my friend John's wedding. I was a groomsman and had to dance one song with a bridesmaid. Of course, they paired me up with a woman with enormous hooters, which were protruding ominously out of her dress. So I am trying to maneuver this woman around the dance floor without making contact with her trophies, as my wife carefully watches. I also am aware that if this chick decides to unexpectedly give me a neck-nuzzle, my life is going to be hell for an indefinite time. No one can be expected to perform well under those circumstances.

My daughter knew the dance could be a problem, so she selected a song that was easy to "shuffle" to. Her expectations may have been low because, my brother-in-law Mike a year before had set the "family" standard for this dance. Mike had actually taken lessons to prepare to dance with his daughter Hannah at her wedding. After Mike danced admirably, and knowing my turn was coming up, the women folk in my family all asked: "Oh Don, are you going to take dance lessons before Cassie's wedding?"

I considered this an outrageous question. Of course I am not going to take any dance lessons. In my opinion, I consider this behavior a violation of the "man code". However, I will grant Mike an exemption because this dance was very important to his daughter. Still, I hold Mike completely responsible for everything that ended up happening.

Mike had indeed raised the bar. So, I needed a plan and the plan was this: I would watch instructional YouTube videos to learn how to dance, and then surprise everyone at the wedding with my outstanding moves on the dance floor.

"This is a swell plan. I've got this!," I thought.

I found several how-to videos and studied how the men smoothly glided their partners around. This looks pretty easy. I've really got this. I really do.

The videos emphasized the importance of footwork. Even though I am not a dancer, I am an athlete so I fully understand the concept of proper footwork. I played basketball in high school and Coach Wendmore taught me the proper footwork for playing low post defense, and I reasoned those same principles would be useful in slow dancing. It's like guiding your partner away from the hoop so you can grab the rebound. Yeah, that's it. I've got this. I really do.

I practiced the steps on the YouTube video to the selected song. I couldn't practice with a real partner since this was going to be a total surprise, so I practiced dancing with a broom. Dancing with a broom is like dancing with an anorexic chick, and anorexic chicks make horrible dance partners. But finally I felt like I was prepared and ready for the big game. I've got this. I really do.

Then the big moment came. My daughter thought we were going to "shuffle", but then I assumed the proper dancing position. She said, "Oh, are we going to waltz!", and then the music began.

We literally got off on the wrong foot. My daughter was surprised alright, but she was not adapting well to this situation. My niece Hannah, who of course knows how to dance, quickly determined the problem and shouted out, "Cassie, let him lead! Let him lead!!!!!!!!!!!!"

But it is not Cassandra's nature to be led, something her new husband will find out about soon enough. So we ventured on in an ugly manner, one side pushing and the other side pulling, but at no time was there any coordination or progress. It was an interpretative dance, which represented how poorly the U.S. government functions today.

I hoped the dance did not look as dreadful as it felt, but those hopes were crushed when the heckling started from the crowd. And those hecklers were my best friends, who someone in a moment of horrendous wedding planning, had been seated at a table right next to the dance floor. When you get heckled by your enemies, you know you are performing poorly. But, when you get heckled by your friends, you know it is horrendous.

It turned out to be one of the worst father-daughter dances ever. Thankfully, the photos make it appear that we actually are dancing well. Fortunately, there is no video of this debacle. There was at one point, but destroying a couple smart phones is nothing compared to having a YouTube video go viral.

This was an utter personal failure. It was one of the worst ideas I have ever had. No, I did not have this. I never had this. I really did not. This was embarrassing. In the middle of this joyous occasion, I felt horrible and I felt like a failure.

And then something totally unexpected happened. It's one of those special moments that you remember forever. Later that evening, my daughter sought me out and took me

aside. I thought something was wrong at the reception that needed attention. Then she said: "Dad, you danced really great. I didn't know you could dance like that. Thank you."
In the world's eyes, I am a terrible dancer.
In my daughter's eyes, I am a wonderful dancer.
While these views are diametrically opposed, only one of them matters at all.

*Postview: After this was posted, several people pointed out to me that a video of the dance existed and told me where I could find it (oh joy!). I have never watched it. To me, it would like watching a video of a horrendous car accident you were in; it would just bring the pain back.*

## Who'll Stop The Rain?
## (The Wedding Chronicles Part 3)

My daughter chose a beautiful facility to have the wedding (which, of course, I paid for). The ceremony was to take place on a gazebo in the center of a man-made lake with the guests seated on shore.

Of course, the risk of holding an outdoor wedding is the chance of rain; and the consequences are worse than listening to Alanis Morissette wailing about rain on your wedding day. So, you start checking the weather every day beginning with the five-day forecast. The five-day forecast in Northeast Ohio is akin to the horoscope; it means nothing but it gets printed, so you look.

The forecast for the wedding day:
On Tuesday: Sunny and beautiful
On Wednesday: Sunny and beautiful

On Thursday: Slight chance of showers

On Friday: Monsoons followed by typhoons followed by downpours.

While the rainfall in June had been the second highest in recorded history, July had been slightly below normal. It would not stay below normal for long.

The evening before at the rehearsal dinner, the facilities manager bragged that they had only had 4 rainouts in 15 years. I wanted to tell her that if she had wanted to keep that record alive, she should have never accepted a large check with my name on it.

As predicted, I awoke Saturday to a steady rain. I checked the radar and it was an incredible green mess.

This raised my stress level and caused me to think irrationally. The song on my internal playlist changed from Alanis to Creedence Clearwater Revival. Who'll stop the rain? I'm the Father of the Bride so I should be able to do something, right? But how can I stop the rain? I post this on Facebook:

**Don Ake**
July 19 🌐

My daughter Cassandra Ake is getting married this afternoon in a planned outdoor ceremony. Will be watching the radar all day. Is there such a thing as a "reverse rain dance"?

Of course, one of my Facebook friends strongly suggested that I pray. Yes, I knew this was an option, but I really didn't want to go "Pat Robertson" on this. Robertson is a famous televangelist. In 1985, Hurricane Gloria was headed right for Robertson's vast ministry in Virginia Beach. He claims he prayed and the hurricane spun back out to sea. Robertson drew much ridicule over this statement, especially from people in Massachusetts where Gloria slammed ashore a short time later.

I really didn't know what to say a prayer to stop the rain: "Excuse me God, just wondering if you could turn off your sprinkler system and maybe just kick it back on tomorrow, please." I felt really stupid praying this, but God more than anyone understands just how stupid I am.

So, the prayers started, the rains continued, and the radar stayed green. As I drove the wedding facility, the rains became heavier. I spent the next two hours staring at the sky and continuing to periodically utter a prayer. It was a Cantonese (as in Canton, Ohio, the closest city to the place) water torture. It would rain hard, and then diminish to a light mist. Just when you thought it might stop, it would suddenly rain harder than it had before.

If the ceremony could not be held outdoors, it would be moved into the reception hall. Yes, a wedding would take place, but it was a much less desirable option. The facility manager said the night before that if it rained, it was the bride's decision on where to hold the ceremony.

The guests started to arrive and huddled in groups under canopies. I hung out with the groomsmen and counted down the minutes to decision time. T-minus 20, T-minus 10, T-minus 5, Blast Off. It was 4 o'clock, the music was supposed to start, and it was still raining. I started the long walk up the hill to the bridal quarters to discuss the situation with my daughter.

I anticipated she would be very sad that the ceremony had to be moved inside. There would be tears. I would need to hug her and give that fatherly speech: "There are disappointments in life... but you have to forget those and think about all the good things." This had to be a command fatherly performance. I needed to get her focused on the moment, not the circumstances.

"We have to decide," I said softly.

She looked straight at me and said sternly, "I'm getting married outside and that's it. Everyone will just have to deal with it."

I recognized the tone, the delivery, and the seriousness of her statement because, of course, she learned how to communicate that way from me. What it means is: This decision is final. You can attempt to change my mind, but you will fail and you will regret trying to do so.

I pulled back the next word I had planned to say. I nodded and said, "All right, we will make it happen," and headed back down the hill.

As the rain hit my shaved-head, I contemplated just how I was going to tell everyone the news. This is one of those rare instances in life where you disagree with a decision yet you still support it 100%. This has to be done either out of blind loyalty or unconditional love; in this case, both applied.

I first told the groomsmen I had been waiting with and their jaws literally dropped. I moved along the edge of the crowd signaling to the rest of the groomsmen what was happening. Then I informed the groom, he was surprised but supportive. Next, I informed the minister. He's one the coolest people under pressure I know. His jaw remained firm, but the eyebrows did instinctively rise. "Okay, we will do that," he replied. It really helped that he is the uncle of the bride; I needed all the support I could find.

Finally, I informed the facility manager. I could tell she totally disagreed with this decision. But the customer is always right and it was my signature on that big check. And besides the decision was communicated in such a way that implied finality. She could have tried to change my mind, but she would have failed and regretted trying to do so.

By that time the news had spread through the crowd, I found this Facebook post from one of the couple's friends (used by permission):

Marie Casper Our friends are getting married in the pouring rain now.
18 hrs

And then we dried the chairs as best we could, got everything else ready, and the ceremony took place … OUTSIDE. I didn't even think again about the rain until I was standing in the receiving line, not five minutes after the end of the ceremony, when it started raining again. That's right it STARTED RAINING AGAIN. At some point, just before the ceremony started, it had, in fact, stopped raining for the first time that day, and it didn't rain during the ceremony except for a very brief sprinkle (so I was told). You see, I was so focused on making the ceremony happen despite the bad circumstances, I had failed to notice the rain had stopped. I think that often happens in life. We keep fighting the dragons long after they have gone away.

So, what did this feel like? It felt like raaaaaain – stopping - on the wedding day. It was the good advice that I decided to take. It's like God showing up at the wedding, right when he needed to be there.

*Postview: I did get permission from my daughter for using her comments. So in this one, I look like a control freak and she looks like the daughter of a control freak. Funny how that happens, right?*

## Things You Should Not Do At A Wedding (The Wedding Chronicles – Part 4)

*Preview: At the time of posting, Russia was at war with the Ukraine.*

### We Are Family?

In the receiving line, I met some of the groom's family who were visiting from the Ukraine. They were all smiling and happy until I enthusiastically proclaimed to them that my wife's family is from Russian decent. Suddenly, they all quit smiling and instead started scowling. I don't think they were picking up what I was putin' down, or maybe they did.

I am certainly glad that we sat the Russians and the Ukrainians at opposite ends of the reception hall or we may  have had the opportunity to view some world tensions close up. On a totally unrelated note, the bartender told me that this was the earliest they had ever run out of Vodka! (Ba Ching, Father of the Bride, Ba Ching!). Was that wrong? Should I not have done that?

## The Coin Toss

During rehearsal, I had an idea to toss some coins in the lake as I walked my daughter across the bridge during the ceremony. The problem I struggled with is that this would constitute a severe breach of wedding etiquette since all attention is supposed to be totally focused on the bride during this time.

But I found a technicality; I reasoned that since this was such a long walk (started at the side and involved four turns) that the bridge was in fact a "neutral zone" and tossing the coins would not be a "neutral zone infraction". So I made a plan to do this, but kept it a secret.

Of course, at the very second I decided to toss the coins high in the air over the lake, my daughter got her heel stuck between the slats of the bridge. (My timing has always been impeccable.) When she desperately needed my help, instead of doing my job I am being a goof tossing coins in the lake. For some unknown reason, she was not very pleased by this "surprise". Perhaps I should have told her my plan beforehand. Was that wrong? Should I not have done that?

## Nothing Goofy To See Here

Near the end of the evening, my family was sitting together at a table when my mother-in-law proclaimed, "Donald Ake, I am so proud of you. I thought you were going to do something goofy during the ceremony, but you didn't!" She had obviously missed the coin toss incident. After the laughter stopped, I had to describe the uncouth act in great detail as she stared at me in disbelief. This was way more uncomfortable than if she had actually witnessed it. Was that wrong? Should I not have done that?

## I Have A Big Butt And I Cannot Lie

During the after-dinner festivities I had a plan to very discretely slither over to Deejay Colin and request the signature song of this blog, "Baby Got Back", the song that has made this blog famous worldwide. I told my friend Freddie about my plan and he thought it was a swell idea, which should have been my first clue not to do it. Most of the time when I got in trouble as a youth, Freddie was somehow involved.

So, I snuck around the back of the dance floor and asked Deejay Colin, "You got 'Baby Got Back' on that thing?" He nodded. I said, "I signed your check." He said, "You got it." And with that, I quickly retreated back to the table where Freddie and I engaged in a Beavis and Butthead type celebration laugh.

After the song ended, Deejay Colin announced: "We have a request from Don Ake, father of the bride (whoops there went my anonymity, he knew my name from introducing me earlier). He wants to hear 'Baby Got Back' (a little more embarrassment please). And I have one rule: if you request a song, you have to get out on the floor and dance to it." And with that, he pushed the button.

Baby Got Backfire! I looked incredulous at Freddie. He laughed hysterically and pointed to the dance floor. So, I headed out to use my "moves like Jagger" and hoped no video cameras were running. Really! Because I didn't know what to do on the chorus, so I bent over and slapped my butt cheeks. When I returned to the table, my friends were red-faced and gasping for air from laughing so darn hard. Was that wrong? Should I not have done that?

## Dirty Dancing

Playing "Baby Got Back" had the surprising effect of "loosening" up the young ladies on the dance floor, and the "dirty dancing" part of the evening began. My middle-aged male friends (who were seated next to the dance floor) took great interest in this occurrence. Freddie exclaimed, "If we danced like that when we were in school, I would have gotten pregnant!" One young woman in a clingy, strapless top danced very vigorously, and my friend Al kept waiting for her top to fall as one might wait for the ball to drop on New Year's Eve. But alas, the spandex of today is much stronger than the elastic of yesteryear, and the top held firm, very firm. I just hope that no one actually ended up pregnant as a result of my song request. Was that wrong? Should I not have done that?

*Postview: Freddie took a video of my "Baby Got Back" dance, complete with the slapping on the butt cheeks. Fortunately, he did not post it on the Internet. My wife and other daughter did view it repeatedly one evening until they had laughed themselves out of breath.*

# CHAPTER 12

# More Muses From The Sports World

Here are more observations about the world of sports, but remember, these are more focused on making fun of sports than the technical aspect of the games themselves. Therefore, everyone should find something funny in every one of these.

The second post, "This Super Bowl Match Up Is Deflating", had to be rewritten because my editor said that it contained too many disgusting "ball jokes". Now I know some of you are now asking "How can you ever have too many disgusting ball jokes?" I understand your confusion, but apparently this is possible. So I castrated this essay and made it more appealing to a wider audience. My editor was pleased with the changes.

## Bad Team Names That Will Turn Your Skin Red

*Preview: Many people are making an issue of politically incorrect team names. If you feel this issue is more important than the first million or so problems in the world in front of it, you have that right. In this piece, I point out the problems with some team names which you probably never noticed. This only includes names in the major leagues.*

People seem to be getting all upset about the names of some professional sports teams. Now remember what sports really are: A group of people (called a team), throw, kick, strike or carry, an object (ball or puck) to a designated location (goal, zone, base) in a restricted space (field, court, rink). Another team tries to prevent the first team from placing the object there. If the team is successful in placing the object in the desired location, it is awarded points. These points, which cannot even be used for free gasoline, have magically been transformed into something that is now deemed worthy of billions of dollars by our culture.

This is not a criticism as much as it is an observation. Please, I have season tickets for two college sports at my alma mater. However, regardless of how you view the sports world, you do have to admit some teams have terrible, really terrible, names. Here is my list of the worst team names in professional sports:

## MLB Baseball

**3rd Runner Up** – (Tie) Chicago White Sox, Boston Red Sox. It is not very manly when your team is identified by their attire.

**2nd Runner Up** – San Diego Padres. Padres spend all their time studying scriptures and performing religious duties. They have no time for recreation and, thus, make lousy baseball players. Plus, they are always tripping over their robes.

**Winner** – Los Angeles Dodgers. This is a great name for a dodge ball team. But a baseball player is supposed to catch the ball, not run away from it. I picture some "girly-man" running across the field, arms flailing, screaming, "Please don't hit me with the ball, please don't hit me!"

## NHL Hockey

**Dishonorable Mention** – New Jersey Devils. Sure, name your team after Satan. If God does really care about who wins, your team is toast in the close games.

**3rd Runner Up** – (Tie) Carolina Hurricanes, Colorado Avalanche. Let's name our team after something bad that kills people. You wouldn't name your team the Denver Diabetes now, would you?

**2nd Runner Up** – Columbus Blue Jackets. Who names their team after formal dinner attire? Why isn't the mascot a preppy wearing a blazer?

**Winner** – Nashville Predators. The use of this word is now almost exclusively for describing sexual criminals. I don't even want to think about what an appropriate mascot would look like, but I sure as hell am not taking my kids to any games!

## NBA Basketball

**3rd Runner Up** – (Tie) Detroit Pistons, San Antonio Spurs. You name your team after a car part or a boot part?

**2nd Runner Up** – (Tie) Miami Heat, Oklahoma City Thunder. Let's name our team after something negative associated with our city!

**Winner** – Cleveland Cavaliers. Don't name your team after an attitude, especially a bad, irritating attitude. This is the equivalent of naming a women's sports team the Boston Bitches. (On second thought that be totally accepted in New England)

## NFL Football

**3rd Runner Up** – New Orleans Saints. The team is named after a song. But there are extremely few saints in the NFL, and any news report that starts out: "The Saint was arrested for possession of" is just plain wrong.

**2nd Runner Up** – Cleveland Browns. The team was named after an old coach. Good thing the guy's name wasn't Rebinowitz! But now you are associated with the color of something that describes how the team has played for the last 50 years.

**Winner** – Well you know where this is going. Yes, the worst name in the NFL is Redskins.

But I don't think the name is racist, I think that it is just plain stupid, really stupid. A team named after a skin color? Would anyone name a team the Blackskins? Try the Yellowskins, the Whiteskins or the Brownskins. No you wouldn't. That would be stupid. Just as stupid as the Redskins. It was a dumb name at the beginning and it is still a dumb name.

However, the team has had the name for 81 years. It is part of team history and is ingrained in the team's culture and tradition. Because sports are so esteemed in our culture, the earnest sports fans treat it like a religion. Changing the name of the team would be akin to telling Christians that the name of the savior will be changing to "Frank".

A few Indians say they find the name Redskins "disparaging" which means to belittle or bring reproach on. But I can think of no better way to bring reproach on yourself than to bitch and moan about something this trivial. If you have survived this "atrocity" for 81 years, guess what, it ain't going to kill you! You are belittling yourself, Chief Whinyass.

But I'm a uniter, not a divider. So I propose a 25-cent "stupidity" tax be placed on every Redskin ticket sold and every piece of Redskin merchandise. The money would go to providing counseling services for people who need guidance about how not to be "disparaged" by this dreadful team name.

*Postview: This piece contains the most politically incorrect statement I have every published and yet I did not receive one complaint – about that statement. However I did receive complaints from several Columbus Blue Jacket fans (perhaps their entire fan base) who were upset about be making fun of the team's name.. Sometimes you can only shake your head.*

## This Super Bowl Match Up Is Deflating

*Preview: Right before the Super Bowl in 2015, it was revealed that the New England Patriots had used underinflated footballs in previous games. This initiated "Deflatgate" and unleashed upon mankind the greatest torrent of "ball jokes" ever. I had to comment on this pressing situation.*

I have a big dilemma on what team to cheer for in this year's Super Bowl.

I do not like the Seattle Seahawks....

They have a snooty, arrogant coach and he has produced a snooty, arrogant team. Appropriately, their logo features a snooty, arrogant bird. In addition, Seattle had the audacity to steal the Professional Bowlers Association from my hometown of Akron. I don't bowl, so you might ask why would I care? Well you see we don't have that much in Northeast Ohio. So when another city steals what we do have, we get resentful. That's why I believe Baltimore is the equivalent of Hell (yes, capital H).

But as much as I dislike the Seattle Seahawks, I dislike cheaters even more ....

It appears the New England Patriots tried to gain an advantage in their previous game by playing with deflated balls. This is disgusting on multiple levels. Football is a very manly game, played by manly men, seeking to place an inflated animal carcass on "special" areas of a field, and be awarded points. Men will literally  crash their skulls together causing permanent injuries in order to move that carcass to its desired spot. So to try to cheat by using a sissified ball is total unacceptable. You are not the "Pats", you are the Patsies.

Unfortunately this news unleashed a deluge of jokes centered on soft, squishy or deflated balls unlike any other in the history of mankind. When all people should be focused on the enormous importance of this game, they are snickering anytime they hear the term "squishy balls".

The weird thing is that women who have no interest in football at all are now thoroughly engaged in the game due to the new emphasis on the player's balls. I find this somewhat enchanting and disturbing at the same time. It has turned even old ladies into a version of "Beatrice and Buffoon-head".

> Buffoon–head: Hey Beatrice, Tom Brady is playing with squishy balls....
>
> Beatrice: Heh heh heh, squish, squish squishy! Heh heh heh ...
>
> This so diminishes the prestige of the game.

Now there is one woman who is not laughing at these jokes, Brady's wife supermodel Gisele Bündchen. Supermodels are not accustomed to having other women make fun of their husband's balls. Supermodels being what they are can select mates which have superior equipment. They like to flaunt this fact to non-supermodels who are forced to get by with the sub-standard guys who are left. Gisele is not going to be happy about Brady's squishy equipment so he may receive a penalty in the boudoir.

You can rest assured that if I was married to Gisele, I would never, ever do anything to make her question the condition of my equipment.

Both the Patriots coach and quarterback deny knowledge of the condition of their balls. This is pure bull$#!+. I know this is a delicate and sensitive area, but a man knows when he is overinflated, he knows when he is underinflated, and he knows when things feel just right.

The NFL is trying to develop a procedure to make sure game balls are properly inflated. I think they need to invent a color-coated football. The ball would turn blue if overinflated, pale yellow if under-inflated and standard brown if ready for action.

I also think they should have NFL cheerleaders check the footballs before the game and get them ready for play. These women have considerable experience handling this type of thing and can easily resolve any under-inflation issues. The problem goes completely away if these ladies vigorously rub down the footballs before the game.

The controversy has even caused concern for this year's Lingerie Bowl. That league is also worried about proper inflation and not just for the footballs. I have offered to go to the game and personally make sure everything there is pumped up properly to the leagues standards. After completing this job, I would be willing to stay and serve as a locker room attendant because that is the multi-tasking, helpful, caring type of person I am.

Because of this cheating and lack of machismo by the New England Patsies, I am going to be forced to watch this game with the level of interest of a librarian watching her only football game of the season at a Super Bowl party. Oh, maybe there will be some commercials with cute cats in them. Perhaps I will try the spinach dip on some organic, whole-grain wafers.

I feel my manhood deflating already ……

*Postview: Yes I did get negative comments on this one. Not from people who thought the original was too "racy", but from football fans that thought this was a poor analysis of the game by someone who obviously never played football. That's right, there are people who take football so seriously that they read this as a serious analysis of the upcoming game. Shaking my head yet again.*

## Wiping Away This Super Bowl Memory

*Preview: If the 2015 Super Bowl did not already have enough controversy, one incident, which was not shown on television, created even more problems.*

Well, the big game is over and it produced the crappiest play in Super Bowl history. And I'm not talking about passing the ball from the 1-yard line either. No, the play in question is Seahawk receiver Doug Baldwin pretending to take a dump in the end zone after catching a touchdown pass in the third quarter. This is so wrong on several accounts. Baldwin had just reached the pinnacle moment of his career. He is standing in the end zone and has just achieved football glory. He does not get 15 minutes of fame, only 30 seconds. But it is highly concentrated fame, with 160 million viewers worldwide watching his every move. And it is at this moment that Baldwin decides he will celebrate his stellar accomplishment, by placing the football on the ground, pretending to pull down his pants, squatting over the ball and mimicking the action of pooping on it.

So his highly anticipated next move was pretending to move his bowels.

Poop! Yes, his statement was poop. His message was poop. Now you didn't see this monstrosity, because NBC quickly cut to another camera when he did the pants thing. Wouldn't you love to hear the production audio on that one? "Cut! He's pooping! He's pooping! Switch to Camera 4 now!!!!!!!!!!!!!!!!!!"

It's hard to understand the mentality of why you would want to take a fake crap while the world is watching. His explanation on why he did this was the equivalent of what a 4-year old might say after taking a real dump on the floor. Fake pooping is not acceptable anywhere out of the grade school playground and even then you make sure no girls are present.

The NFL was not pleased. It is rumored the NFL Commissioner took a real sh!+ in his pants after Baldwin's antics. Baldwin was subsequently fined $11,025 for the incident. Reportedly, the extra $25 was for industrial butt wipes to clean the spot he left on the end zone. Perhaps Baldwin got confused by the term "end zone".

As disgusting as this was, there is a much bigger issue at play. The Super Bowl is not anything about poop. No, it is totally non-poop. It is the anti-poop. I am guessing there is less poop produced while the Super Bowl is played than at any daytime period during the year.

Nobody wants to poop during the Super Bowl. You could miss the big play, and there is no way to inconspicuously slip away and do your business during this game. And for sure you don't want to poop when you are attending a Super Bowl party for fear of stinking up the host's bathroom:

*I forget who won the 2011 contest, but wasn't that the year we had to watch the rest of the game in the garage and burn candles because Joe took that nasty dump at halftime?*

Not having to poop during the game is part of a fan's pregame preparation. You make sure you get plenty of fiber and drink plenty of water, so your game-day poop takes place in the morning and you are thoroughly cleansed by kick-off. Unfortunately, with 160 million people involved, there are probably millions of people who need to poop during the Super Bowl but hold it in until the game is over.

So, the Super Bowl is the ultimate no-poop event. That is why there are no laxative commercials, no adult diaper commercials, no fiber commercials and no toilet paper commercials during the game. And especially no commercials for prescription drugs like this one: "Side effects may include: explosive diarrhea, green poopies, humongous stools and sh!+ing brick-like objects."

In the End Zone

So the danger of doing a poop dance during the Super Bowl is immense. It would be the visual equivalent of a brown note (a hypothetical infrasonic frequency that would cause humans to lose control of their bowels due to resonance. SOURCE: Wikipedia).

If Baldwin's poop dance would have been shown, millions of viewers who were trying to hold it in until the end of the game would have simultaneously filled their pants. I'm sure some people, who did see the "poop dance" live at the stadium were injured racing to the rest room to secure a stall.

That's why there is no place for any mention, any reference, and especially any displays of pooping at the Super Bowl. It needs to remain a totally poop-free zone.

Unfortunately, thousands of Seattle Seahawk fans still ended up sh!++ing themselves at the end of the game, but that is the price of making a call that bad. Everyone was concerned about the Patriots under-inflating their footballs but no one expected the Seahawks fans to over inflate their underpants at the end.

*Postview: I preformed somewhat of a public service here since many people were not aware of the fake pooping incident until they read this post.*

## You Should Not Mix Sex And Golf

*Preview: Sometimes you see headlines on the Internet that you just must check out. This story is funny enough on its own, but I felt the need to provide a unique perspective on the situation.*

A Playboy model and a radio show host are involved in a lawsuit regarding a golfing-related incident that occurred in 2012. Liz Dickson agreed to lay on her stomach with her buttocks exposed while Kevin Klein hit a golf ball that was atop a tee that was placed between her butt cheeks. (I am not making this up).

This gives a whole new meaning to the term "tee box" and it has to be the extreme example of "improving your lie". However this is so wrong on so many levels.

Now I know women will not understand why a man would even think of doing this. But if a guy comes up with an idea that results in a beautiful woman lying at his feet with her tush exposed, that is what is referred to in the book of "man rules" as a "winner". In addition, this stunt combines sex and sports interacting together. Golfing involving Playboy models is close to nirvana for some men.

But there lies the problem. Golf requires total concentration. It requires you to focus squarely on the target. Unfortunately, when faced with a golf ball teed between the buttocks of a Playboy model, there is confusion about what the true target is. The male brain has difficulty handling this type of information. Of course, the male brain consists of the Upper Processing Unit (UPU), which handles almost all functions and is logical and rational. How-ever, there is also the Lower Processing Unit (LPU), which is totally focused on matters of the "procreating" variety. Unfortunately, the LPU has the ability to totally shut down the UPU when it deems it necessary. This golf shot creates severe conflict between the UPU and the LPU.

In addition, this is considered a "trick shot" and presents some golfing challenges. First of all, the ball is much higher than if it were teed on the ground. To compensate for this, the swinger should choke up on the club. However, "choking up" is not considered manly and would lessen the machismo factor of hitting a ball off the bare buns of a hot woman. Secondly, you could use less club. But when trying to impress a Playmate, you want more club, not less club. Playboy models like bigger clubs, so you are going to whip out the biggest club you got. Under the circumstances, I believe a wedge would have been best, but Klein used his huge Ping.

The other problem is that even with the ball teed up, he was not hitting off a "flat" surface. As research for this post, I had to carefully examine photos of Miss Dickson. While she is a very beautiful woman, if she were a golf course, she would be known for her impressive "back nine". And while curves on a golf course can make shots difficult, Dickson's curves made this shot a real challenge.

So it should be no surprise that with all these factors in play that Klein took a strong, healthy swing. Under normal circumstances, you would have said he "grounded" his club. Of course, in this case that meant he struck Dickson square in the ass. This resulted in Dickson suffering "severe injuries", some of which are "permanent". As a result, Dickson is suing Klein for $500,000.

Of course, I am siding with Miss Dickson. You might say she deserves what happened because she was stupid enough to participate in these shenanigans. But I say Playboy models are expected to display their wares, be entertaining and pleasing to men, and that is exactly what she was trying to do.

And I believe $500,000 is a fair price because Klein literally damaged a "masterpiece". This was a work of art, and I have heard art critics in this realm say that "Good ass is hard to find."

I hope that Miss Dickson prevails and recovers from her injuries. I don't know much about therapeutic massage, but if Miss Dickson needs someone to tend to her physical therapy needs, I would be willing to lend a hand for absolutely no charge. That's just the type of guy I am.

*Postview: This was one of those posts that many people Googled after reading to make sure that I didn't make it up. There is absolutely no enhancement needed for stories like this!*

# CHAPTER 13

# More Crazy Economics

THE IMPORTANT THING TO REMEMBER HERE IS THAT SOME of the posts do deal with serious subjects: Bad banking practices, horrible government regulations and an important presidential election. I just choose to explain these topics in offbeat, creative ways. Again, you should get a chuckle even if you slept though economics class in school. Enjoy!

## Bankers Gone Wild! – Watch Them Flash Your Cash!

*Preview: The banking crisis of the late oughts (00's) was caused by banks making risky investment contracts known as derivatives. The largest and most ridiculed bank involved in this was J.P. Morgan Chase, whose CEO is Jamie Dimon (so J.P., Morgan and Jamie). TIPS (Treasury Inflation Protected Securities) is a type of investment.*

Cue some wild party music …..

Host 1: Welcome to another exciting episode of "Bankers Gone Wild". Today, we are going to follow the wild hijinks of J.P. and her two banking buddies Morgan and Jamie as they party in the exotic Derivative Islands.

Host 2:  Yes, the Derivatives are a dangerous, yet exciting, place for wild bankers to frolic. There are shark-infested waters and many places for naughty financiers to get into trouble.

Host 1:  Looks like the girls are getting very drunk on a combination of cheap money and greed.

Host 2:  Wow, that's a lot of loose cash. I just hope they are able to control it!

Host 1:  Oh no! They've started buying! Whoa, look at them buy. It's like they are just buying anything. Buy, Buy, Buy!

Host 2:  Those girls are really moving that cash! They are awesome! They are totally out of control!

Host 1:  Oh no! They have started to really lose it.

Host 2:  Yeah, they are really wasted. Isn't it great?

Host 1:  No, I mean the cash. They are losing it. They are wasting it big time. This often happens when investing in the Derivatives.

Host 2:  Wow, they are losing every time! Lose, lose, lose. Those losses are really racking up!

Host 1:  They've just blown through a trillion dollars! Maybe we should say something.

Host 2:   Girls, you've lost a lot. Maybe you should slow down a bit.

Host 1:   Oh no! They don't care. Now they're flashing us their assets!

CENSORED—CENSORED—CENSORED

Host 2:   Hey, they're right back at it.

Host 1:   Look at all that cash. It's flowing right down that rat hole! Lucky rats!

Host 2:   Here we go again. Lose, lose, lose!

Host 1:   These bankers have gone super wild!

Host 2:   Look, they just blew through their second trillion, and now they are lying exhausted on the beach.

Host 1:   Hey, girls. You just lost two trillion dollars in the Derivatives. Aren't you even a little embarrassed? What do you have to say for yourselves?

Host 2:   What's that? You say it doesn't matter because you still have plenty of cash. Oh great, here we go again. Now they are flashing us their balance sheets! Look at that bottom line! Look at those TIPS!

CENSORED—CENSORED—CENSORED
!!!!!!!!!!!!!!!!!!!!!!!!!!!!!!!!!!!!!!!!!!!!!!!

*Postview: I cut off the last part of the post because it was a serious commentary on the banking crisis, and we certainly don't want any of that staid garbage here. However, this post is the second most popular post ever of my economic blog.*

## The Economics of Underwear

*Preview: I love finding unusual economic indicators and then try-ing to find out if they have any validity. Hey, I get "up close and personal" in breaking down men's underwear sales.*

In December, I listed men's underwear sales as an un-usual economic indicator. This indicator was first developed by former Fed head Alan Greenspan in the 1970's. My initial thought was that the men's underwear market is much more complex now, and so I questioned if this was still a valid indicator.

I couldn't find an update on men's underwear sales, so I started thinking about my own underwear purchases over the last three years:

- 2008 – The economy was still strong and I had plenty of disposable income. I purchased six pair of underwear. It was the most expensive underwear I have ever purchased in my life. It was underwear that is sold on individual hangers, not in packages. It was colorful, it was flashy, and it was totally un-necessary. My wife is not going to be impressed by my choice of underwear after nearly 30 years of mar-riage. I don't have a hot, young girlfriend. And the underwear looks "slightly" out of place on my aging, baby-boomer body.

  So why did I buy it? Because I could. My underwear selection is representative of the wildly conspicuous consumption and over-the-top spending that char-acterized the years prior to The Great Recession.

- 2009 – The Great Recession was in full gear. My disposable income was gone due to job loss. I bought no underwear, even though the pair I was wearing when they told me I was downsized had to be destroyed.
- 2010 – The recession has ended and a subdued recovery has begun. My disposable income is still low; however underwear is still a necessity even in these times. I do not recommend "going commando" to save money and it is certainly not acceptable attire for job interviews. I agree with Kramer on this one, "my boys need a house".

However, after a year of no underwear purchases, some existing inventory is wearing thin. So I recently have made my first underwear purchase in almost two years. But did I buy the fancy, high-priced stuff on the hangers? Of course not, but I was able to purchase very good underwear at a closeout store. This underwear cost 70% less than the ones I bought in 2008. Why was it sold at closeout? Because the maker of this formally expensive underwear went out of business when the recession hit. His sales were dependent on people having significant disposable income to spend on "high-end" (not tight end) underwear.

And that's why this recovery will be subdued. People are not going back to their previous uninhibited buying habits either by necessity or choice. This recovery is being led by cheap underwear!

*Postview: Oddly enough, my readers, including women, enjoyed this discussion of my underwear buying habits.*

# This Sugar Substitute May Not Be Very Sweet

*Preview: Bad government policies result in a potentially damaging substance to be included in many of our foods. Not funny, but of course I can make it be!*

**(I am co-authoring this post with Dr. Reginald Sheeply, Professor of Economics at Scotland University.)**

Last summer I vacationed in Hershey, Pa., home of the world-famous Hershey Chocolate Company. And while my family was fascinated by all the chocolate, I was fascinated by the company's marketing, quality control standards and deep commitment to American manufacturing. I was also inspired by the story of Milton Hershey who finally was a huge success in the candy industry after several devastating failures.

We ended our day at "Chocolate World" with a visit to one of the largest candy stores in the world. We are all "kids" in that candy store. There must be a hundred different types of chocolate, in addition to other candies sold by Hershey.

After hearing numerous times during the day about the commitment to domestic manufacturing, I looked at the label on a package of Jolly Ranchers (a brand acquired by Hershey in 1996) and saw the words "Made in Canada"! What in the name of Milton Hershey is going on here?

It all has to do with the economic "Law of Unintended Consequences" which states that actions by individuals and especially governments often result in unanticipated effects.

In the 1980's, some congressman convinced his colleagues to enact high tariffs on imported sugar to preserve the jobs of domestic sugar beet farmers. I believe he accomplished this very difficult feat for one of the following reasons:

A. He was a very skilled congressman

B. Many other congressmen owed him a big favor

C. He had compromising photos of the Speaker of the House and a farm animal.

Dr. Sheeply, what do you think about this if it was in fact reason "C"?

"That's baaaaaaaaaaaaaaaaaaaaaa aaaaaaaaaaaad."

This sugar tariff which is still in effect has resulted in the following:

- **Higher Sugar Prices.** Sugar prices are much higher than they should be. It is in effect a tax on sugar that is estimated to have cost U.S. consumers around $2.5 billion in 2009. A sugar tax? Where have you heard that before? Oh that's right; the British enacted the Sugar Act on the American colonies in 1764. It was one of the taxes that led to the Revolutionary War. I guess back then we got upset, now we just blindly pay it.

Dr. Sheeply, what is your opinion of high sugar prices? "They're baaaaaaaaaaaaaaaaaaaaaaaaaaaaaaaaaaaaaad."

- **Unintended Job Results.** The high sugar tariff is preserving the jobs of sugar beet farmers; however, the unintended consequences have been significant. Products that use high amounts of sugar, Jolly Ranchers for example, cannot be competitively manufactured in the U.S., so every one of those jobs moved to Canada or Mexico. It is difficult to measure the exact impact on jobs, but it very well could be a net job loss.

In addition, it puts every domestic manufacturer that uses sugar in its products at a competitive disadvantage against imported products and limits export sales. Sugar prices are very important to chocolate manufacturers. Ironically, two of Milton Hershey's early business failures were caused when sugar prices spiked. The Hershey Company survived because Milton solved the problem by growing his own sugar in Cuba. Milton Hershey would despise the sugar tariff.

Dr. Sheeply, what do you think about losing jobs due to high sugar prices?
"That's baaaaaaaaaaaaaaaaaaaaaaaaaad."

- **A Questionable Substitute.** Because sugar prices were so high, Coca-Cola and Pepsi started using a new sugar substitute called High Fructose Corn Syrup (HFCS). This sweetener is derived from corn using a special manufacturing process. There would be no market for this product if sugar was available at the free market price.

The problem here is that several credible medical studies have found there are possible health concerns in how HFCS is processed by the human body. This impact is much more prominent in men than it is in women.

Of course the corn farmers and HFCS producers have run television and radio advertisements promoting the naturalness and wholesomeness of the product.

Remember, these are some people who think that burning corn as fuel in our cars is a great idea.

So who are you going to believe: medical scientists who are trying to keep us healthy and have no financial interest in the research findings or people who are making billions of dollars off the product?

I don't know the answer, but it is a moot point with me. You see this one is personal. I have two health conditions that I am currently taking herbs and vitamins to control. The medical studies say the main two health concerns with HFCS are the two conditions I have. I am the canary in the coalmine on this one. If the studies are accurate, HFCS will kill me before it kills you. So I obviously try to limit my HFCS consumption as much as possible. People always laugh at my McDonald's meal of Quarter Pounder, large fries and Diet Coke.

Dr. Sheeply, what do you think about HFCS?

"It's baaaaaaaaaaaaaaaaaaaaaaaaaaaaaaaaad."

Therefore, policies by my own government may be "poisoning" me, and my government is making me pay more to do this. It's enough to make someone a Ron Paul supporter.

*Postview: Every time this issue is raised in Congress, it never comes up for vote. It dies a slow death, similar to my pancreas.*

## Swimsuit Model Economics

*Preview: This economic indicator is real, but real stupid. I do love the disclaimer.*

**Warning: The following post contains statements of a strong heterosexual nature and other statements**

**that could be considered "sexist". Reader discretion is advised.**

> Well the Ukraine girls really knock me out
> They leave the West behind
> And Moscow girls make me sing and shout
> That Georgia's always on my my my my my my my my
>     my mind (The Beatles)

I stumbled upon another unusual economic indicator this week. It is the "Sports Illustrated Swimsuit Issue Indicator". It says that when an American appears on the cover of the swimsuit issue, stocks do well that year. But when a foreigner appears, the stock market drops.

This year's cover model is Russia's Irina Shayk (she is just a few letters short of being an Austin Powers character). According to the article I read, this is bad news for the stock market. Although it is uncertain how bad it will be (the author actually ran a historical analysis based on country origin), since this is the first time a Russian has appeared on this cover.

Of course, this is silliness and has about as much credibility as Groundhog Day predictions. But Irina is more interesting to watch than Punxsutawney Phil, so of course it deserves much closer study all in the name of economics. So what does the selection of Irina Shayk say about the economy and the stock market this year? Who better to analyze this than I?

**Stability.** When I heard the woman was from Russia, I expected to see a pale, lithe blonde. But Irina appears healthy, solid and stable. Not quite a "brick house", but she's no pushover. For someone living in a tough Russian economy, she is not malnourished (of course, she doesn't lack for dinner invitations, does she?) But she has recovered nicely from the recession. She is getting three square meals a day which are being converted into some impressive curves. After the turmoil of the past years, we seek substance and stability.

**Genuine.** Irina is not even a light-skinned blonde. She is a dark-complexioned brunette. She is not overly sexy, just very beautiful. A natural beautiful with no fillers, supplements or enhancements needed. After all the phoniness we've just experienced, we desire something real.

**Long-Term Perspective.** Irina is not a woman for a one-night stand. She is a woman for the long haul. Again, beauty trumps sex appeal. After all the get rich-quick schemes of the oughts (00's), we want long-term investments. You may have flipped houses, but you wouldn't flip... (Okay I'm not going there)

**Functionality.** Irina looks like a baby-maker, or in today's lingo a baby-mama. She is a strong, well-built woman, with nice childbearing hips. She looks capable of popping out a baby on Tuesday and being back working in the fields on Thursday. Because of course that is what Russian women have had to do throughout history. And obviously the babies will be well fed. She could even manage triplets I bet. Sure there would be a waiting line, but nobody would go to nap time hungry. We now seek things that are productive and make sense.

**Strength.** Russian women are very physically strong. They are stronger than they look. It's in the DNA. Anyone who's watched Anna Kournikova crush a tennis ball can attest to that. Correction: anyone who's actually watched her tennis racket strike the ball can attest to that. We now seek strength in our institutions (and our cover girls).

**Intelligence.** I'm guessing here but, I believe Irina is probably very intelligent. I am basing this on the fact that I personally know four Russian women, and they all have three things in common. They are very intelligent, very charming and very beautiful. Think about it. All those Russian spies in the movies weren't just beautiful, but they were crafty and smart. Hey, wait a minute. Maybe I should not have shared all those proprietary company documents with Svetlana who just happens to work for a competitor. Rats, taken advantage of again! We seek intelligence after listening to the fools.

**An Economic Indicator.** So looking at all these factors, I think the choice of Irina does have indications for what we want in our economic future. And it's surprising that a Russian woman has not appeared on the cover of the swimsuit edition before. Of course, back when it was the U.S.S.R., commie girls were such a turn-off, unless you were the Beatles.

And if Irina happens to read this and wants to meet to discuss economics, I will gladly listen to her opinions. The Model T (the original name of the economics blog) meets the Model I.

*Postview: I enjoy this one because I was about to take a silly subject, make it even funnier and inject serious commentary at the same time. Not very easy to do!*

# We're Shakin' Cause
# The Economy's Not Bakin'

*Preview: In the 2012 Presidential election, Americans had to determine which candidate would do better leading the economy. I tried to simplify it for people. Note: "Mittens" was a nickname (sometimes used in a derogatory manner) of Mitt Romney.*

"Good evening, this is Eugene Roush reporting from the World Economic Speedway. There is much excitement here because in just a few weeks we will find out if there will be a new driver of the U.S.A. car or if people will decide to stick with the current operator. I am joined today by renowned NASCAR driver Ricky Bobby of Talladega Nights fame."

| | |
|---|---|
| Eugene: | First we are going to talk to current driver Bearleft Orama. Bearleft, how do you think you have performed as a driver the last four years? |
| Bearleft: | I have driven the car just great. I've put my foot on the accelerator and kept the car on the right course. I am an excellent driver and absolutely deserve to continue driving for the next four years. |
| Ricky Bobby: | How fast you driving this thing? |
| Bearleft: | I'm doing around a 1.3 GDP. |
| Ricky Bobby: | 1.3! I can go faster than 1.3 riding naked on a tricycle! |
| Eugene: | Now don't exaggerate. |
| Ricky Bobby: | No really, I have. Want to see the photos? |

| | |
|---|---|
| Eugene: | No!—Bearleft, why are you going so slowly? |
| Bearleft: | The previous operator of the car ran it into the ditch and caused considerable damage. Me and my team had to repair it, and now this is all the faster it will go. |
| Ricky Bobby: | That sounds like you are making some wimpy excuses. Are you sure that's all the faster it will go? |
| Bearleft: | Look, I'm trying really hard and I care deeply about going faster. I know I'm not driving as fast as the Chinese car, but just give me more time and I know I will drive much faster. |
| Ricky Bobby: | Trailing the Chinese? That's disgraceful. Look dude, if you ain't first, you're last! |
| Bearleft: | Let me be clear: I am a great driver. If you don't believe me, just ask me or anyone on my team. I'm the best there is, plain and simple. When I wake up in the morning, I whiz excellence. |
| Ricky Bobby: | Hey, that's my line! (Actual line from the movie: I p*** excellence.) |
| Bearleft: | Not anymore. I'm the king of this track! |
| Eugene: | Now let's talk to the man challenging Bearleft for the opportunity to drive the U.S.A. car for the next four years, Richie Richney. |

| | |
|---|---|
| Ricky Bobby: | Those are interesting drivin' gloves you got there. |
| Richie: | Oh these aren't driving gloves; these are my silk driving mittens. They're from France! |
| Eugene: | Are you sure the people will accept a driver wearing such expensive "mittens"? |
| Richie: | Why not? Underneath the mittens, my hands are human, just like theirs, although with a much better manicure. |
| Eugene: | Do you think you can drive the U.S.A car faster than 1.3 GDP? |
| Richie: | Are you serious? My grandmother could go faster than 1.3 GDP. In fact all 12 of my grandmothers could drive faster than that! |
| Ricky Bobby: | 12 grandmothers? How is that even possible? Your grandfather must have been a real tomcat! |
| Eugene: | Why do you believe you would be a better driver than Bearleft Orama? |
| Richie: | I've had lots of experience driving smaller cars on other tracks. I drove the Bain car and had it zooming really fast. I drove the Olympic car to victory and I once drove the Massachusetts car on the American circuit. |
| Eugene: | How are you going to get the car to go faster? |

| | |
|---|---|
| Richie: | I plan to put high-octane fuel in the tank and to take off all the restrictor plates. |
| Eugene: | Can you give us more details? |
| Richie: | Uh, no I can't. |
| Eugene: | How about you Bearleft, what is your plan? |
| Bearleft: | Plan? I don't really need a plan. Remember, I whiz excellence. Just watch me! |
| Richie: | Oh yeah? I can whiz excellence too! Only faster! |
| Eugene: | Run Ricky Bobby! It's turned into a giant whizzing contest! |
| Ricky Bobby: | Shake and Bake! I just wish I would have brought my raincoat! |
| Eugene: | Ricky Bobby, what happens if neither Bearleft Orama or Richie Richney can drive the U.S.A car any faster? |
| Ricky Bobby: | Then it's time to pray to that little baby, in that little manger...... |

*Postview: Hey, you can be the judge if the right choice was made, but the car has never really run very fast in the succeeding years. I think everyone would agree that the end of the 2012 campaign did turn in to a giant pissing contest!*

# CHAPTER 14

# More Holiday Cheer

T HE ESSAYS IN THIS CHAPTER CAN BE ENJOYED ANY TIME of the year. This stuff happened at Christmastime, but the underlying themes involve dealing with difficult co-workers, shopping at the mall and eating pudding. Also included is a horrendous, year-end reflection.

## A Very Heartwarming Christmas Miracle Type Of Story

*Preview: Even though we are adults, we still love good stories, especially Christmas stories. Here is a Christmas story for adults.*

Gather round children. (Okay, children shouldn't be reading this.) So gather round grown-up children. Your Uncle Don is going to tell you a heartwarming Christmas story that truly expresses the meaning of this glorious time of year.

Many years ago, on a morning just a week before Christmas, Uncle Don's butthead boss called the whole marketing department together for an important announcement. It seems the evil bean counters had completed next year's budget and determined that in January, one person would have to be dismissed from the department.

You might wonder children, why oh why, would the boss announce this right before Christmas? Why not just wait until January to deliver the news to the unfortunate individual, and let everyone enjoy the holidays in peace? Well children, that's why he was a butthead. He was a big 'ol stu-  pid butthead who often just farted out random thoughts for no good reason. You will find that many managers you encounter in your career are buttheads, with a big butt right where their brain should be.

After the announcement, the workers were dismayed and scurried down the hall to discuss the situation. They could not believe the company would do this because it was making plenty of money, and the department was overworked already. Everyone was in agreement this was a bad, bad thing.

And this was a strange occurrence because it caused Uncle Don and Val the Bitch to agree on something. Val the Bitch and Uncle Don did not get along very well at all. Val the Bitch hated Uncle Don and was threatened by his superior marketing skills and vast intellect. Uncle Don hated Val the Bitch because she was a stupid, disgusting mega-bitch with a horrible personality and no marketing skills whatsoever. And that's the honest to goodness truth, children because Uncle Don would never lie to you.

Her bitchy personality and lack of physical attractiveness resulted in her having serious problems in her social life. Several times a year, she would arrive at the office and announce loudly and enthusiastically, "Hey, I got lucky last night!" What that really meant children is: "Hey, I'm not such a disgusting bitch after all. I had a boyfriend last night for 10 minutes!"

Yes children, this behavior was typical of the disgusting, pathetic existence of Val the Bitch. But don't think that Uncle Don wasn't sympathetic on these occasions. He wondered just how desperate, lonely, drunk, insane or stoned a guy would have to be to actually copulate with Val the Bitch. He hoped these unfortunate souls were not emotionally (or physically) scarred for life. And most of all, Uncle Don hoped that they took a long, hot shower using industrial-grade soap as soon as they got home because it is difficult to wash that type of bitchiness off of you.

But now Uncle Don and Val the Bitch were suddenly on the same team, united in scorn of the butthead boss. As the discussion wound down, somebody realized that the butthead boss had chosen to make his announcement a mere 90 minutes before he was taking the department out for our annual festive Christmas lunch. What moronic timing! That puts the butt in butthead.

"Merry Christmas," said someone sarcastically.

"Merry Frickin' Christmas," said Val the Bitch.

"Merry Frickin' Christmas indeed," exclaimed Uncle Don.

So, the Christmas lunch was very awkward that year. The Christmas joy had been sucked out of the employees, but the butthead boss was having a great time yucking it up, totally oblivious to the lack of enthusiasm of all the others.

After the meal, the butthead boss raised his glass in the air with great fervor and bellowed, "Merry Christmas!" Of course at that point everyone else thought in their heads, "Merry Frickin' Christmas." Unfortunately, your Uncle Don started to laugh at this thought and lowered his head so he would not fizz off the boss with this highly inappropriate outburst.

And it was at this moment something magical happened. Val the Bitch, who happened to be sitting next to Uncle Don, gave him a swift, hard kick under the table. This immediately snapped Uncle Don to his senses and he thrust his glass in the air and proclaimed: "Merry Christmas indeed!" With this, the Christmas luncheon and Uncle Don's job was saved. It was a miracle children; it was a Christmas miracle!

And then in that restaurant, in that moment of Christmas merriment, Uncle Don realized that Val the Bitch was not really a bitch at all, but was a valued co-worker. She was a real person with real feelings and real issues and she was trying to do the best with what she had. And this children, is the miracle of Christmastime; when everyone puts away their petty grievances and learns to love their fellow man. Where there is peace on Earth and goodwill to all men, which does include all the bitches and bastards in your life.

Merry Christmas Children and Happy Holidays from your Uncle Don

*Postview: I had actually worried that someone would take exception to the term "Val the Bitch", but nobody did. I think we prob-*

*ably all have had that one co-worker (man or woman) who falls into this category.*

## A Holiday Shopping Wonderland

*Preview: This was posted shortly after Christmas 2014. Sony Corporation's emails had been hacked reportedly by North Koreans.*

I made my annual trip to the mall this Christmas. We think we are very sophisticated, complex beings, but play some Christmas carols (audio stimulus) and shine some Christmas lights (visual stimulus), and we are drawn to the mall like rats to the cheese. Of course there is some good cheese at the mall, usually packaged with a tasty beef log. Mmmm, beef log.

Surprisingly, the mall wasn't that crowded. I assume more people were shopping on-line this year, maybe because of all the credit card fraud at some major retailers. When online shopping is the safest option, you know there is a big problem. I was going to buy a Sony television, but I was afraid my personal info would get hacked and I would end up also buying Christmas gifts for thousands of North Koreans. A "North Korean Christmas" (Oh, let's see what Little Kim Jong-un got this year!) might make a heartwarming Hallmark movie, but it would be a horror movie when I opened my credit card statement.

## Shopping In The Cloud

My first stop was Yupperman's department store. The perfume cloud at the front of the store was so thick this year that it coated my body. Normally, I would be concerned about arriving home reeking of perfume, but this is the expensive stuff worn by classy ladies. My wife knows that women this refined would not be cavorting with the likes of me.

I think I figured out why these stores create the perfume cloud. Once guys get coated with this stuff, they may feel more feminine and be tempted to become transvestites. "Hey, I'm already wearing women's perfume; maybe I should get some women clothes!" You may scoff, but the women's clothing section is located next to the fragrances. Coincidence? I think not. Don't worry; it did not work on me. Yupperman's clothing is much too classy and expensive for a cheap tramp like me.

## Please Just Shut Up

At my next stop, the perky sales clerk insisted on explaining the Super Duper Customer Loyalty Program in excruciating detail. The program is about as complicated as quantum physics and twice as boring. As far as I can tell, the program has something to do with earning "points". But as a guy, the only points I care about are how many Ohio State scored in the Sugar Bowl, which are 42, and how many points are prominent in the latest Jennifer Lopez video, which are always "2".

## Camping Out At The Mall

I had problems navigating around the calendar kiosk because some guy decided he would park his baby stroller in the main aisle. Only this was not a traditional stroller, it was a baby Winnebago. It had enough storage space for a camping trip to the Alaskan wilderness. I can't imagine a baby owning enough stuff to store in that contraption; perhaps these people shop at Yupperman's. I just hope they eventually donate the stroller for housing to a homeless person (and his family).

I was surprised the daily calendar "What Your Poo Is Telling You" is still very popular. I was again tempted to buy it, but realized that it would be giving me shit every day this year, which very accurately describes my previous job. No, I've already lived that year and never, ever want to do it again.

## Keep No Secrets

I did not shop at Victoria's Secret because it's not a good place for middle-aged guys. If the size is too small, you get no sex. If the size is too large, you definitely get no sex. If the size is correct, but the style is wrong, you still get no sex. It's just too risky. I also try to avoid stores where the saleswomen wear push-up bras. Would you like the matching feather scarf with that, it's only $50 and it looks oh so sexy, purrrrrrrrrrrrrrrrr?" Push-up bras = pushed up profits. No, this is a store for the younger, clueless guys who are actually going to get sex, regardless of what they buy.

## I Lost My Head Over This One

I was very offended to see that the male mannequins in one department store were all headless. This is highly insensitive considering recent world events. If we make mannequins already without heads, then the terrorists have won! Either that or the store is implying that men are brainless when it comes to fashion decisions, so women need to buy them some decent clothes. And, we all know that is so not true.

## I Skipped The Free Food Sample

But the weirdest thing I saw at the mall was this Asian guy handing out food samples in front of the Japanese food stand Wok This Way in the food court. I noticed that he had this strange, slightly angry expression on his face and I wondered why. I think the guy was in fact half-Asian but was contorting his face to appear full-Asian. He probably thought he could hand out more samples if he looked more authentic and I do admire his dedication to his job.

Of course, I cannot fully describe exactly what he was doing without being extremely offensive and horribly politically incorrect. You will have to figure this one out on your own since I would not want you to have a slanted opinion of me.

*Postview: This is why I only shop at the mall a couple times of year. I end up doing more people watching than shopping. I consider it one of the strangest environments in our culture.*

## Buttheads, Buffoons and Bitches That Made 2012 Special

*Preview: I still don't know why this particular year was so weird. I was encountering goofheads everywhere and decided to chronicle these events in one post.*

This year would have been much better if I had not encountered a series of idiots, morons and buffoons. So I've decided to dedicate the last blog post of the year to the people who fizzed me off the most in 2012.

I know I have previously posted about other people who upset me during this year, but in those cases there was an element of humor in the story. The following things are not funny when they happen to you. But they didn't happen to you, they happened to me. So enjoy!

Here are my Fizzed Off Awards for 2012:

**4th Place – A Facebook Fudgehead.** A "Facebook" friend insisted on posting extreme political nonsense on his wall during the presidential campaign. I don't believe in using Facebook for political debate, but I did post one video of a parody containing footage at a political rally. I posted this because it is hilarious, not because it was political. But my fudgehead friend took exception to my post and I really took exception to his exception.

Two days after the election, I received a poorly done, homemade political poster sent anonymously in the mail. However, I don't associate with anyone so juvenile and moronic that would do such a stupid thing. Well, except one. So CRAIG, I know you sent it. That's right CRAIG, I know it was you! You think you are smart CRAIG, but you are too stupid to realize how stupid you really are! (I know you are confused by the last sentence, so maybe you should read it again). Yes CRAIG, because you are such a moron, you really fizzed me off this year.

**3rd Place – Stan the Aggressive Cemetery Salesman.** Stan the cemetery salesman was determined to sell me a burial plot this year. When I asked him to call back in three months, he called back in two weeks. He left numerous messages on my answering machine. Finally, he called and spoke to my wife and she blasted into him and told him never to call again. When my wife is this upset, her communication is crystal clear. There is absolutely no ambiguity and no chance of a misunderstanding. I have avoided needing a burial plot up to this point due to being able to understand (and obey) my wife's heated communication.

However, Stan is an imbecile. He called back a few weeks later on a Saturday morning when my wife was still in bed. I knew that if I did not take action, I would be the object of my wife's wrath in a few minutes. So I explained to Stan in very graphic terms (without swearing!) what would happen to him if he ever called my house again. This was effective, but we did have to replace our phone because part of it melted during the conversation. Stan, you really fizzed me off this year.

**2nd Place – Ditzy Editor.** A major, local newspaper (not in Akron or Cleveland, so you figure it out) wanted me to write a new economic blog for their website. They made a major error in setting the blog up by not asking my permission to post some of my old content on the new blog site. This led to one reader complaint. The problem could have been very easily resolved, but instead they shut down the new blog immediately without even informing me.

It took five days and two e-mails (she didn't even call me to discuss the matter) to find out what happened and why. And then she told me that I was responsible for the incident even though it had been her gross incompetence that caused it. I explained in an e-mail (she never returned my phone calls) how she was totally responsible for what had happened and why, but I never even received an apology. I can't believe that someone in her position could be so densely incompetent and unprofessional. What a useless piece of dukey. Ditzhead, you really fizzed me off this year.

**1st Place - The Ticket Bitch.** I received a letter telling me that due to a previous purchase I could get free tickets to an outdoor lunch before a sporting event. I followed the instructions in the letter, but the organization failed to mail the tickets. So my wife made a special trip to personally pick them up. After she got home, she realized the buffoons had given her the wrong tickets. They were to a similar event that day. So we had followed their instructions to the letter, but they had screwed it up twice.

When we got to the event, the Ticket Bitch wouldn't let us in to the lunch. When I tried to explain what happened, the Ticket Bitch repeatedly interrupted me to tell me what mistakes I had made and why my tickets were no good. I had other documentation that proved I qualified for admission, but the Ticket Bitch would not even let me complete one sentence. Finally, the Ticket Bitch said that even though I was at fault, she would grant me access to the lunch. I wanted to go nuclear, but I was hungry. The Ticket Bitch could not understand why I was still livid after she had most graciously let me in. It's because you are a bitch of enormous proportion; you are a horrible, disgusting MEGA-BITCH. I pity your husband and family, Ticket Bitch. And you really fizzed me off this year! Congratulations on your first place finish!

Happy New Year to all my readers, and please don't fizz me off in 2013!

*Postview: I really don't find this post very humorous, but my readers loved it! People also enjoyed the use of the word "fizz" versus the colloquial alternative. It actually made the piece funnier. After this post, several people greeted me by saying: "Now Don, I don't want to fizz you off" ...*

## Getting Figgy With It This Christmas

*Preview: My solution to putting the joy back into Christmas because of course I love pudding. My children claim they are going to choose my rest home based on the quality of the pudding they serve.*

The Christmas celebration has begun, but we are leaving something out of Christmas that is very important. Something that was once an integral part of the holiday is now missing. Something that is so essential to the day that if it were reinstated it would transform the culture and make Christmas the joyous occasion it once was.

Of course I am talking about pudding. Back in the old days, and by old days I mean the 1500's, pudding was a key part of Christmas. As evidence, I present a couple of verses from the Christmas carol, "We Wish You A Merry Christmas":

> Now bring us some figgy pudding,
> Now bring us some figgy pudding,
> Now bring us some figgy pudding,
> And bring some out here.
> We won't go until we get some,
> We won't go until we get some,
> we won't go until we get some,
> So bring some out here.

You notice that these people are demanding, not politely asking, for figgy pudding. And this is not negotiable, because they won't leave until "we get some" (which interestingly is Lounge Lizard Larry's strategy at the single's bar on a Saturday night). These guys in the 1500's were getting "figgy" with it.

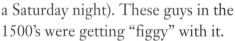

Old recipes for Christmas pudding have been passed down (maybe on ancient, sacred scrolls) from the pudding makers of yore. From these nearly medieval manuscripts, we find that pudding masters would combine the most expensive, delicious ingredients into a holiday delicacy. But over the years, the significance of pudding at Christmastime has faded into oblivion.

And what Christmas traditions have replaced the pudding? Consider these:

**Bargain Campers.** These morons camp out for four days so they can be first in line to get cheap stuff at the electronics store. Hey idiots, consider this: if your time is of such little worth that you can waste four days "camping" on concrete, you don't need a new big-screen TV. You need a new life! And you can't buy one in that store!

**Brawling Shoppers.** Have you seen the video of the guys wailing on each other at the Victoria Secret store on Black Friday? Nothing says Merry Christmas like a punch in the face. When men are fighting over women's panties and there is no actual woman in those panties, there is something seriously wrong.

**Gift Cards.** Giving a gift card means that I did not take the time to try to figure out what you might want or need as a gift. Neither did I make the effort to drive to the store, make a selection, and stand in line to pay for it. No, here's a cheap piece of plastic. Now you go and buy your own #!*$ing gift! Merry freaking Christmas!

**Lame Christmas Music.** There has not been a good Christmas song written in years. This causes radio stations to play Mariah Carey's, "All I Need For Christmas Is You", 50 times every day in December. Overexposure to this song is the number one cause of people tossing their Christmas cookies. No, we desperately need some new songs and those songs should all be about the joy of eating Christmas pudding.

**The Solution.** All this crap has sucked the real joy right out of Christmas. The best way to put the joy back in is pudding because there are few greater joys in life than eating delicious homemade pudding. Instead of loading up our credit cards with enough debt to last us to August, we should load up our bellies with scrumptious Christmas pudding made from the finest ingredients available. We should all make pudding and then invite our neighbors and friends over to enjoy it. This would make Christmas a special time once more.

Putting pudding back in Christmas would revolutionize the holiday. I believe even atheists would celebrate Christmas if it involved several days of pudding eating. Heck we may pick up a few Jews and Hindus, too.

So people, let's get figgy with it once again and start putting pudding back in Christmas (and do it right here!). And while you're at it, don't scrimp on the good tidings.

*Postview: Sadly my attempt on improving Christmas failed miserably. I really thought my pudding idea might catch on. Of course then someone would put a big pudding store at the mall and ruin everything.*

# CHAPTER 15

# More Miscellaneous, Diverse, Random, Ramblings

HERE ARE MORE RANDOM THOUGHTS ON SUBJECTS AS DIVERSE as swingers, beards and North Korean first ladies. I am an equal opportunity humorist. I don't discriminate. I just dissect, looking for fun in all the wrong places.

## Funny Business at the Comedy Club

*Preview: I really don't know how I get myself in so many weird, bizarre situations. A combination of unlikely circumstances combined to produce a night I will never forget.*

Several weeks ago I made my first visit to a comedy club. I went to see my friend Chuck Costanzo who was the opening act. (Yes, I have a friend who is a stand-up comedian, so I probably do think that I am cooler than you) And when I visit new places, you know strange things are going to happen and this night was no exception.

It is a comedy club, but not all the funny business was happening on stage.

Soon after I arrived I noticed a young woman who apparently had left home that evening in a big hurry. I say that because she had forgotten to put on the rest of her clothes. She was there in her undergarments. They call them undergarments because they are meant to be worn "under" other garments called outer garments. I must say that it was a very nice corset, but unless you are paid to swing on a pole, you shouldn't be wearing one in public.

My guess is that she is a Lady Ga Ga wannabe. Obviously she doesn't realize that even Lady Ga Ga would wear a dress to a comedy club. And unfortunately beauty-wise this woman was no Lady Ga Ga. She was a little chunky monkey. There were "deficiencies" that she should have been trying to conceal, but the junk in the trunk was all out there on display like a human yard sale. And, made you think that this junk could be obtained very cheaply. No need to undress her with your eyes, she had done if for you. I gave her the name Lady Gag-me.

Soon a couple, Ben and Lorrie, were seated at my table. They were an attractive couple in their late 30's and seemed like very normal people. However, almost from the beginning Lorrie began flirting with me. Now at my age, when a younger, attractive woman flirts with you it is much appreciated. But, I was getting a bit uncomfortable especially since Ben was sitting right there hearing everything. But he didn't seem to mind it. In fact it looked like he was actually enjoying it. So Lorrie made even more suggestive comments and kept giving me very seductive looks.

Finally, Ben apparently took exception to something Lorrie said and announced how he was going to "discipline" her for that comment later that night. I thought he might be joking, but the wicked smile on Lorrie's face told me he was serious. Later in the evening, Lorrie did lean over and whisper to me exactly what she had planned for Ben later that night.

After the evening was over, I realized that I had actually participated in a "threesome". This was Ben and Lorrie's verbal foreplay and I was the foil. Of course, I was never invited to participate any further in this "game", which is a good thing because I am "definitely not into that". But don't feel bad for me. If I really wanted some affection, I'm sure Lady Gag-me needed a ride home.

As this conversation was happening I found it very bizarre, but now I find it highly amusing. The only reason that I was exposed to these shenanigans is that I was attending the show with my friend Bob, who is also a friend of Chuck's. I was expecting to arrive late, so Bob was supposed to get there before me and get a table up front. But apparently Bob had trouble reading the e-mail I sent him explaining what time to arrive and also had trouble understanding my instructions when I called him the night before to make sure he would get there on time. So Bob was late; very, very late. Leaving me to be a foil for the verbal hijinks of this horny couple.

The comedy actually occurring on the stage was awesome. Chuck (see photo) did a great job with his routine, which included a bit on how great it would be if women could produce beer instead of breast milk. A woman at the table next to me said she would give it a try and several guys immediately volunteered to be taste testers.

The main act was an Arabian comedienne with huge breasts and she was hilarious. I found myself becoming attracted to her because I am a former stand-up comedian and I appreciate her talent. It had nothing to do with her breasts, which are enormous. Her jokes were really funny, especially the ones about her large, heaving, breasts.

Overall, it was a very enjoyable evening. The packed crowd really got into the show. Ben and Lorrie did leave in a hurry shortly before the show ended. I guess they had something else to do, can't imagine what it was. I hoped they enjoyed the show, but even if Ben didn't, I know his evening had a happy ending.

*Postview: After posting this, people did not believe this happened. They thought I was making it up or had interpreted the circumstances wrong. Even Bob didn't believe me and would not back my story up. By the time he entered the picture, I had stopped responding to Lorrie's flirtations. So, she started jokingly putting me down in an attempt to force me to reengage the conversation. Bob just thought that was humorous and innocent. However, soon I would have some concrete evidence of what happened that night.*

## Swinger's Night at The Comedy Club

*Preview: I posted "Funny Business at the Comedy Club" on Chuck Costanzo's Facebook wall because I had written about his comedy routine. Obviously, Chuck is tied in to the local stand-up comedy scene and is Facebook friends with all the area performers. One of Chuck's fellow comedians then dropped a bombshell that changed everything.*

### *Now it all makes sense ..... sort of.*

*After writing my last blog post about my weird night at the comedy club, a friend of Chuck Costanzo (one of the comedians) read the blog post and left a comment on Facebook about members of a "swingers convention" in attendance the night I was at the show. This explains a lot.*

**I Am Not Making This Up.** My friend Lori (not the same Lorrie from the club) has accused me in the past of making my stories up. Well Lori, I really hope this proves to you that I don't. No, I am not a fiction writer. Unfortunately, this does prove just how bizarre my life really is. Who walks alone unbeknownst into a room full of swingers? Who does that? I believe that I could have my own reality show because my life is so utterly wacked out. I could keep up with the Kardashians. Okay, I couldn't keep up with the sexual activity of the Kardashians, but what human could? Maybe a rabbit on a good night. But my stories are basically true. I do admit that some are enhanced with a bit of literary Viagra, but I only do that to firm up the humor. And this story was not enhanced!

**Advice From An Old Friend.** After reading the post, my good friend Grace chastised me for attending the show without my wife. Grace has been chastising me since our high school days. This proves two things: I am still a goofball and Grace hasn't changed much either.

But I don't think her opinion on this subject is valid. I shudder to think what might of happened if my wife was with me that night. The couple at our table may have thought we were new members of the swingers group. If Lorrie said the same things to me that night with my wife present, there would have been some serious swinging. I would have hoped that Lorrie was into S&M, because she would have experienced some serious pain. It would have been difficult to explain to the police, however.

**Things I Now Understand.** I evidently was sitting right in the middle of the swingers group. I found it odd that many of these people seemed to know each other, but were not socializing with each other. I now know why. You've heard that having sex with someone can ruin a previously great (platonic) relationship (remember the Seinfeld episode). So in the swingers' world, doesn't it reason that having a friendly relationship with fellow "participants" can ruin great sex?

I also now understand "Lady Gag-me", who was no doubt part of the swingers group. If you are accustomed to being naked around and having sex with strangers, then wearing lingerie in public is really no big deal. Maybe the outfit was strategic in that she could be the first one naked at the group meeting after the show. Remember, the early bird gets the, um, worm. Now you might consider that cheating, but uh, that's the whole point, isn't it.

**One More Incident.** There was one additional incident that night that didn't make sense at the time. There was this hot blond prancing around the club in a very short skirt. I assume she was part of the group. I was worried that if she sat in the front row with her legs crossed, that Chuck might get distracted and mess up his routine. But apparently Chuck is a professional who is able to stare at a hoo-hah and make people laugh at the same time.

However, when I was leaving the club, blondie was engaged in a conversation and was partially blocking the narrow hallway leading to the back exit. I walked up to the opening and stopped, needing her to move so I would be able to pass through. She stopped talking, looked right at me, and then resumed the conversation without budging an inch. Now I could make it through the opening, but not without making some contact with her bodacious booty.

So, I now have three options. First, I could tap her on the shoulder and ask her to please move so I can get through. This is the only option if this is a guy blocking the hallway and I'm sure the option that my friend Grace would prefer. I could "back" through the opening so any contact would be cheek to cheek. And of course I could scoot through front first. I won't reveal which option I chose, but I will say I left the comedy club that night with a huge smile on my face – and that's the whole purpose of going, right?

The following describes how I felt that evening:

(Parody of "Stuck in the Middle with You" by Gerry Rafferty and Joe Egan)

> Well I not sure what is going on here
> I made friends fast but I starting to fear
> Yeh this chick is really hitting on me
> I just wish she'd stop squeezin' my knee
> Swingers to left of me
> Swappers to the right
> Here I am, stuck in the middle it's true ………

*Postview: Well, this made the first post even funnier. And now most people believed my story was true, but incredibly Bob still doubted me—until we went back to the club.*

*A year later, the same comedienne was back and Chuck was opening for her again. Bob and I went back for the show. Except this time, I decided to take Grace's advice and we took our wives. We got a table for four, and Bob and his wife even got there before us because Bob's wife actually knows how to tell time.*

*Chuck introduced me to the comedienne (name withheld by request) before the show, and I told her about my experience a year ago. She did find it funny, but I could tell she was not surprised. She then told me that for some strange reason people practicing "alternative lifestyles" tend to really like her act. She told me the same swingers group had attended the early show the day prior. The same show I had of course attended last year. (I swear that during this conversation I did not look at her gigantic breasts even once)*

*I went back to our table and told everyone the new details. Finally, Bob realized I had been telling the truth. Now he understood how stupid I looked. He started laughing until he was literally red in the face. The stand-up comedy was excellent again, but Bob never laughed that hard the rest of night.*

## Always Use Some Horse Sense When Choosing a Wife

*Preview: This post is from July 2012. U.S. Secret Service agents had just been caught entertaining call girls in Columbia.*

***Note: None of the details presented in this post are made up. That's right; sometimes the truth is just that funny!***

The Internet news organizations were sent into gyrations a few weeks ago when North Korea leader Kim Jong Un was seen in a photo with (GASP!) a woman. But not just any woman, she was a "mystery" woman. Not to worry, the South Korea intelligence service sprang into action to find out all they could about this chick. This means either they don't have enough to do, or they are some very horny guys, or both.

Unfortunately, the U.S. could not send agents over there to support their efforts after the Columbian call-girl scandal. Having our guys spy on beautiful, young women is just asking for trouble, and let's face it, too darn expensive.

The South Korean agents quickly identified the woman as Hyon Song Wol, a singer known for the hit party songs; "Footsteps of Soldiers", "She is a Discharged Soldier" and "We are Troops of the Party". Yep, great party songs, Communist Party songs. No indoctrination going on there! But

Wol's greatest hit was "Excellent Horse-Like Lady" released in 2005.

Now, of course this is disturbing. I have always questioned the North Koreans' taste in women since the year  2000 when 63 year-old Secretary of State Madeline Albright made a diplomatic trip there. The North Korean leaders all wanted to dance with her because they thought she was hot! Hell, Madeline Albright wasn't even hot when she was 23! There is something really wrong here. So if the North Koreans think Maddie was a babe, they may just take a second look at ol' Nelly.

I have never thought about comparing horses to women. Sure I appreciate sleek, shapely legs. But I prefer only two, without hooves, please. And what guy doesn't value a set of championship caliber hindquarters? But that is as far as it goes.

However when I watched the "Excellent Horse-Like Lady" music video (yes there is one), it showed three happy, very attractive (no horsing around here) women working in a factory. So it is excellent to "work" like a horse, but not look (or even smell) like one. Therefore, it appears maybe the North Koreans are making progress in evaluating female beauty.

But then the shocking news came out that the mystery woman was not Hyon Sol Wol, but really Ri Sol Ju. Then the news reports started to appear in rapid succession. This was the hottest topic on the web:

"We just found out that Kim Jung Un likes Ri Sol Ju" (three minutes later)

"Wait, she is really his wife!" (five minutes after that)

"And they have a 3-year old son!" (seven minutes after that)

So Kim found a woman, got married, and had a three year-old son all in the span of 15 minutes! And you thought North Korea was behind the times!

The good news is that Kim has made an excellent choice and Ri does not resemble a horse. She does not have a "long-face". In fact, a North Korean man interviewed for a news report said she has a "round face" and clear skin. Her legs are shapely, hoove-less and not overly hairy. Unfortunately there are no photos available to adequately evaluate her hindquarters, but she is a former cheerleader so we can assume that there is no capitalist junk in that trunk. The guy interviewed for the news report also said that Ri makes an excellent image of an obedient, comrade wife and she even "wears colors"! Booyah, Kim! Booyah!

Kim's father had four or five wives, so Kim is well on his way to collecting a fine stable of fillies. And because he is 28, likes video games and is in control of a nuclear arsenal, we want him to get all the mane and tail that he wants.

We want him very happy – and exhausted - every night, if you get my drift. So my advice to Kim is "Giddy Up!"

*Postview: Interest in this subject was so high in Asia and Australia, this post is the seventh most popular "Ake's Pains" ever. Giddy Up Indeed!*

## Duck Dynasty Beards Make You Smarter

*Preview: I think I have uncovered the secret behind the popularity of the show "Duck Dynasty" and the beard craze in this post from October of 2013.*

Duck Dynasty is the most popular "non-scripted" show on television. Every week, millions of people tune in to watch the escapes of these self-proclaimed Louisiana rednecks. Now I am a big fan of the show, but I have figured out the major reason for the show's success: It's all about the beards.

I know Duck Dynasty has many popular themes and characters, but if you took away the beards you would have no show. If the characters looked like New York yuppies or clean-cut Mormons, no one would watch. But because these guys have such huge beards, people think everything they say is inherently wise. How else do you get away with saying things such as:

- "Them berries are the nectar of the earth. God put them here so we could have their juices. Their sweetness is unparalleled"; or
- "Dealing with family is a lot like eating squirrel. You end up getting very greasy, but in the end it is worth it."

These beards also have mystical powers. How else do you explain the many women who send fan mail and marriage proposals to Uncle Si? This guy looks ragged, has poor eyesight and readily admits to having bad hygiene habits. You have to assume that at least some of his female fans have all their teeth and that a few are actually hot.

I think big beards are making a comeback because it makes men appear smarter than they actually are. Remember the photos of the old scientists in your school textbooks. You read that "Ivan Von Gorkney discovered the element Mahowidum," and you thought "Of course he did, look at the size of that beard! That guy is really smart!"

And look what has happened since our Presidents stopped wearing beards. Our last bearded leader was Benjamin Harrison in 1893. He was no genius, but he probably was better than some of the clean-shaven goofs we have had recently. However, I do not recommend that President Obama grow a beard because he could end up looking like one of those old communist guys and we would never want that!

I got to see the power of a big beard close up through my friend Shamus (this is the last time I let anyone choose their own pseudonym. You are such a tool, Erin. Whoops!) Shamus took great care to grow his huge, bright-red beard. He even used two different beard conditioners and a special shampoo to get the desired rich, fluffy look. I think his morning beard grooming is similar to the effort that Farah Fawcett put into her hair back in the 70's.

Shamus works as a salesman and his power beard made him a dynamic sales superstar. Customers always were glad to see him and his beard visit them. His company featured his face (and beard) in its print ads. He and his beard were on fire. His sales sky rocketed. Shamus was by far the best salesman at the company In addition, women would stop him at Wal-Mart and ask if they could touch and stroke his beard. Many of these women had all their teeth and some were in fact, hot.

But then summer came and Shamus decided to shave the beard. Suddenly, his customers were too busy to see him. His company decided to feature a ferret in its advertising instead of him. His sales started to slide big time. And women, including his wife, ignored him. So of course he grew it back. He told me, "The beard is back and it is angry." The beard is now so popular, he is considering getting it its own Twitter feed: "Looking pretty good after the morning shower. Trim to follow."

Because apparently beards make you appear smarter than you actually are, I decided I should change things up. Many people do not fully appreciate the existential wisdom that is extruded from my vast cranium. I believe that a beard might help people realize just how astute I really am. So I took some Rogaine, mixed it with some steroids, and then threw in some Viagra to promote length and started a diet of sea urchin and tree bark. This photo shows the result. Now I'm looking pretty wise, don't you think?

*Postview: I actually have some people ask me if that beard was real. I also had people comment that I looked more like a terrorist than a "duckie".*

# CHAPTER 16

# More Celebrity Diatribes

Just because someone is beautiful and/or talented does not mean they are intelligent. Celebrities often do stupid things, and with the myriad number of "news" agencies on the Internet, we now get to know "everything" about everyone. So when someone is, or does something, especially stupid, I go to work.

## Jennifer Lawrence's Photos
## Do Not Include Me

*Preview: In September 2014, Jennifer Lawrence's phone account was hacked and nude photos and videos were leaked online. Why a beautiful celebrity has to have nude photos and videos is a mystery to me. To impress or attract a guy? Come on, you are Jennifer Lawrence! And what about being a celebrity and having a flimsy password on your phone? Duh and double duh.*

In response to media reports regarding the hacked and subsequently leaked nude photos and videos of Jennifer

**251**

Lawrence, this is the appropriate time for me to issue an official statement.

Despite what is being reported by TMZ, Entertainment Tonight, Access Hollywood, The Weather Channel and others, I am not the person seen with Ms. Lawrence in several of the photographs. I categorically deny ever engaging in the shenanigans displayed in the pictures, and especially the video.

I must point out that Ms. Lawrence has also strongly denied having similar contact with me. It is somewhat disturbing that Ms. Lawrence has not denied being with any of the younger, buffer, better haired men in some of the photos, just me.

I admit that the guy in the leaked materials bears a striking resemblance to me; but I assure you it is a case of mistaken identity. I also acknowledge that the person in the photos has a distinct birthmark on a personal part of his body and that TMZ is reporting that I have a similar birthmark. But this evidence comes from an old schoolmate Ronnie Myers, who says he remembers the alleged birthmark from the showers after junior high gym class. Why he would even remember this is his issue.

I may have met Ms. Lawrence one time. I mean I do get around, but frankly I just don't recall the encounter. I know she has admitted meeting me, but I'm not surprised knowing the impression I tend to make on people and the sheer popularity of my blog. I really don't know Ms. Lawrence and that is why I am referring to her as "Ms. Lawrence" and not "Jennie-poo" like the guy in the video, who purely coincidently sounds a lot like me. Also, nothing should be concluded from Ms. Lawrence referring to the guy as "Bloggerstud". I think this is a total misrepresentation of the audio.

The guy may be German and she may be using a Germanic reference, like blugerstad or something similar to that.

Somehow Access Hollywood got hold of my cell phone contact list. I do admit there is a Jennifer Lawrence on that list. She happens to be my dental hygienist. I do realize there were a significant number of texts exchanged between me and this Ms. Gardner (who I have called "Jenny" on several occasions, but again never, ever Jennie-poo). The reason for all the texting is Ms. Lawrence is a true dental professional and she was just checking to make sure I was flossing and taking proper care of my teeth. In addition, any uses of the word "oral" in these texts were in reference to oral health. Also any references to "getting drilled" and "filling cavities" were strictly dentistry related.

You should also ignore the statements from my attorney claiming that I am owed royalties if these photos or videos are used for commercial purposes. He is speaking in the weird language of "legalese" which no one really understands. How would I expect to get any money from this when it is definitely not me in these photos? I just wish the paparazzi would leave me alone (see photo).

Finally, please disregard the threats issued to me by Jennie's, I mean Ms. Lawrence's current and former boyfriends, and she has had a bunch of them. You would think she would be a little more selective don't you know? I think these guys are just trying to be macho and they see no risk in threatening an older, distinguished gentleman like me.

Chris Martin of Coldplay has threatened to shove his guitar up my "c clef". I don't know if that is possible, but I am selling my front row seats to the Coldplay concert next month. I don't even remember who may or may not have given me those choice tickets.

So the one thing to remember is that once again I am totally innocent of anything anyone accuses me of at any time. You may now resume believing anything else you may read on the Internet.

*Postview: This post is the tenth most popular "Ake's Pains" at this time. I saw a business associate who had read this post shortly after it appeared and he asked me if I had ever met Jennifer Lawrence. I was surprised by the comment, so I laughed and answered "No." Now I believe a more appropriate response would have been: "No comment."*

## Dr. Oz Is Full Of It

*Preview: This post questioning the accuracy of Dr. Oz's advice appeared in August 2013, a full year before a medical study claiming he is correct less than 50% of the time was released in December 2014. Then there were people on the Internet calling for him to resign in April 2015.*

*So this post was way ahead of its time, a trendsetter so to speak. I may not be a doctor, but I went with my gut, and sometimes my gut is pretty smart!*

One of our biggest multi-media authorities is this guy Dr. Oz. Dr. Oz is this medical doctor who apparently is smarter than any doctor who ever lived. He is also smarter than all the doctors alive today. Dr. Oz gives a variety of advice on any and all medical and health issues and it is all absolutely, positively, completely accurate! We know this because Oprah Winfrey says it is true. And Oprah is the closest being we have to a modern day Buddha. Dr. Oz has so much great advice that he needs a television show, books and a web site to be able to proclaim it all.

So it may come as a shock to millions of people around the world that due to my vast medical knowledge and education I have determined that: DR. OZ IS FULL OF S**T!

Here is my evidence:

- Dr. Oz obviously is from the Land of Oz, which means his medical license is from Oz and this is one wacky place. I suspect that there were some weird medical experiments being conducted in Oz. Think about it. The Tin Man had his heart removed, but still was able to function. The Scarecrow had his brain removed but was still able to speak. The Lion was male, but lacked courage. This probably meant they had cut off his, ah, ozzies.

This is why much of Dr. Oz's advice sounds as if it came from monkeys flying out of his butt. This stuff may work on

Munchkins, but not for real people in the real world. Just like the Wizard, Dr. Oz will be exposed to be a fraud. Pay no attention to the man in the white coat because: DR. OZ IS FULL OF S***!

- Dr. Oz wrote an article saying all the things your mother did to treat your childhood ailments were wrong and did not really help you at all. So Dr. Oz thinks he knows more than my mom about medicine cabinet treatments. Really, really, Dr. Oz?

Whenever I was sick or needed any treatment, my mom did just the right thing to make it better. Mom told me I would get well and I always did. So if Dr. Oz thinks he knows more than my mom about making boo-boos heal fast, then: DR. OZ IS FULL OF S***!

- Women listen and believe Dr. Oz because he is a good-looking doctor. Chicks dig doctors cause they have loads of cash and it's just a bonus if they are considered cute.

I first heard of Dr. Oz when my co-worker Shelia announced that she had gone orgasmic because of this "doctor" she watches on television. I asked her if her husband was enjoying this and she said her husband was not joining her in this activity. When I inquired further. she told me it was all about orgasmic foods. I ended the conversation at this point because whatever she was doing with any cucumbers because of Dr. Oz should not be discussed at work.

Regardless, the choice of a healthcare professional should never be influenced by their appearance. Of course, an obvious exception is made for Swedish nurses, which I recommend their treatments be applied to my body whenever I get a headache. So even though women love him: DR. OZ IS FULL OF S***!

So to review: Dr. Oz thinks he is brilliant. Dr. Oz says lots of medical stuff. But in reality: DR. OZ IS SO, SO FULL OF S***!

*Postview: This post was only mildly popular when released. However, it became very popular after the study was released. Some people even posting things with the exact same title at that time.*

## Kim's Bum Is A Master-Piece

*Preview: When Kim Kardashian claimed she was going to "break the Internet" by posting a photo, I had to look, right? And I was not prepared for what I saw, so of course I had to, as a public service, write about it.*

Naturally I was very concerned last week when I read Kim Kardashian was threatening to "break the Internet". You know how much I hate Kim Kardashian, and you also know how much I love the Internet, so this was of supreme interest. And because security of the Internet is essential to me doing my job and earning an income, I immediately stopped all work to investigate this dangerous threat.

I soon learned that Kardashian's evil plan consisted of her posting a nude photo of her oiled bum. I needed to literally get to the bottom of the issue, so I clicked on the pic.

It is impossible to describe this image with mere words. As the photo engulfed my 21-inch, HD monitor, I sat in stunned awe. Just as you cannot adequately describe fine art, I am not able, nor am I worthy to expound about this bum. However, this is even more awe inspiring than mere artwork. It is a naturally occurring wonder, similar to the beauty of the Grand Tetons. Her bum is smoother and rounder than the Tetons, yet just as large. Yes, Kim Kardashian's bare bum inspires the same reverence as viewing the most prodigious natural wonder.

However, these bodacious buns are worthy of careful examination, much like a classic sculpture. Kim's bum is not to be ogled; it is not to be leered at. It is to be carefully gazed at, much as art connoisseurs tremble in the presence of the most beautiful sculptures in existence. One must appreciate the curves, the smoothness and the solid, rock-like quality of this most exquisite derriere. It is a masterpiece – a literal master piece.

This bum is so incredible that I don't consider it pornographic; it is by all means pure art. As attractive as it is, it does not stimulate me to want to make love with Ms. Kardashian. In fact I believe it would be dangerous to engage in such activities. One wrong move, one unanticipated shift, and you and your man parts could be crumpled under the force of that powerful bum. I'm sure some of Kim's lovers have been crushed to death and removed from mattresses by the Jaws of Life. Of course, she paid to have the tragedies covered up.

I think like other heavy construction jobs that making love to Kim is a two-man job. I am not advocating group sex per se. One man would be dedicated to the main task while the second man would be in control of positioning and managing that prodigious bum. They would need to communicate by Wi-Fi headsets to safely complete the task:

"I've got it stabilized! Now shift slightly to the right, then push, that's it, push again!"

I would also recommend all future lovers receive certification training before being permitted to enter her boudoir. Paramours would also be required to be equipped with GPS in case they got trapped in the crevasse. It would also help if you had experience traveling around the Australian countryside, especially the outback and the bush lands. . An oxygen supply is necessary in case you got trapped underneath.

This, of course, means that Kanye West is in grave danger. However, many people do not consider that a bad thing. I do not think Kanye can control that bum. In fact, I think that bum controls him. For example:

Kanye: Let's eat Mexican tonight!

Kim: No, my bum says that Mexican can irritate her. She wants Chinese.

Navigating Kim's body would be quite an accomplishment, and I'm sure the feeling would be similar to climbing Mount Everest. I'm sure conquerors feel like planting a flag pole there. Perhaps I should rephrase that: They feel like showing some physical representation of their accomplishment!

Even though Kim has made millions off her derriere, it is literally her "money maker" (and it is so impressive she doesn't even need to shake it). It does have its drawbacks. Her clothes are custom made – no one makes size 5X booty with 120-degree curves. Her toilet seat needs shock absorbers. When she has an itch, she needs a team of ass-scratchers all with smooth fingernails. And she needs to live in a sturdy, reinforced, house because when gas passes through that thing, it shows up on the Richter scale.

I am still not a fan of Kim Kardashian, but now I am a huge admirer of her bum. If her bum ever creates a Facebook page, I will "Like" it. I will send it a "friend request" and hope it accepts me. Maybe then the bum and I can chat occasionally. I think I would really enjoy that.

Fortunately, the photo of the big, beautiful oiled Kim Kardashian bum did not break the Internet. Unfortunately,

 keeping the image on my monitor for an extended period of time while I studied it very carefully for art's sake of course totally shattered my monitor. But it's a small price to pay to view one of the wonders of the modern world.

*Postview: I could write an entire blog on the escapes of the Kardashians, but then I might actually begin to care about them and that would be wrong.*

## Joe's Prostate Has A Problem

*Preview: When a former professional athlete's fame, influence and marketability start to wane, they end up doing commercials they really should not do.*

I was watching a very manly sporting event on my big screen when suddenly former NFL quarterback Joe Theismann appears with some extremely disturbing news. Joe is very upset and seems to be in serious pain because of his prostate. He then goes on to describe in excruciating detail how his prostate has swelled to enormous proportions and the problems this is causing him. (The graphic represents how irritated his prostate is)

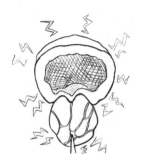

When Theismann was quarter-backing the Redskins, he had a very athletic prostate. It was the type of prostate that would hang in the pocket and not get jittery, a prostate that could thread the needle and perform at a very high level. But now his prostate is weaker, bloated and unpredictable, and prone to spraying errant passes all over the field.

And because Joe is concerned about his prostate, he thinks you should be very concerned about yours also. If his NFL quality prostate has deteriorated this much, imagine what condition your fat, lazy gland is in. This did make me very concerned. It also made me want to run to the bathroom because I had just finished a large birch beer.

But now suddenly Joe is smiling because his prostate is very happy. He found these magic pills to shrink and control his prostate. It turned his dominant alpha prostate into a passive super-beta prostate, which just sits quietly in the corner until you need it. No need to see your doctor about the problem. Who are you going to trust, some quacky geek or a pro quarterback?

But I did feel very uncomfortable watching a former great athlete talk so vividly about a personal issue. I want to remember Joe Theismann running for a key first down, not running for the first toilet he sees.

**And Then It Happened Again.** A few days later, former gymnast Mary Lou Retton, the darling and gold-medal winner of the 1984 Olympics, is on my television screen and she also has a problem. It seems that all that stretching, pressing and doing power splits have loosened up Mary Lou's plumbing. Her pipes have greatly widened with age and are now leaking.

This is very disappointing to all the men who were big fans of Mary Lou years ago. She was the perfect female gymnast. She was pretty, she spoke English, she was very flexible and she even had breasts! Guys fanaticized about helping Mary Lou practice balancing on a beam, exercising on the floor and of course, nailing a dismount.

Fortunately, Retton has found some super absorbent pads to help contain her problem. She does seem happy with this solution, but I would still not attempt any vaults or splits without a cleaning crew standing by.

Retton is still very attractive, but I don't need to know about her personal issues. It is a real turn-off. I want to remember her for scoring a "10" on the floor exercise not doing "number one" all over the carpet.

**And Then It Got Worse.** I already thought this trend was out of control when Tony Siragusa interrupts my T.V. show. Siragusa was an NFL lineman for 12 seasons and was the epitome of masculine machismo. He was a hulking, strong, giant of a man. But now, he also has a personal problem. He is committing what amounts to illegal procedure in his underwear. His solution is to wear inserts, a partial diaper if you will. Sirugusa used to be one of the best guards in football, but now he is putting guards in his underpants.

I want to remember Siragusa as a tough guy who breaks through the opponents shield to sack the quarterback, not some guy who has to carry a sack of soiled shields out to the trash. And the worst thing about this is: HE IS NINE YEARS YOUNGER THAN I AM!

I am not making fun of these medical conditions, which are very serious and that afflict many people, including my friends. What bothers me is that my former sports heroes are revealing very personal issues that I don't need, nor want, to know. This is way too much information for me. This is making me so upset that I am close to p*$$*ng my pants, ah, uh wait, what were those things called again, Siragusa?

*Postview: Thankfully I don't think any of these commercials is still running, although the Siragusa one had the longest "shelf life". However there are new ones airing with other celebrities that are just as bad.*

## Snooki is Pregnant

*Preview: The third "poem" in the book!*

Snooki is pregnant
She's growing a kid
It is not a result
of something I did

I was not intimate with Snooki
I did not propagate her nookie
I did not visit the Jersey Shore
I did not tap the Jersey whore

Snooki is pregnant
She's growing a kid

It is not a result
of something I did

*Postview: You mind find it strange that I choose this stupid, little poem as the last post in the book. However, this one is very significant because it was almost the last "Ake's Pains" ever.*

*When that local newspaper decided to run my economics blog on their website (Chapter 14 - Buttheads, Buffoons and Bitches That Made 2012 Special), I had decided to stop writing "Ake's Pains". There was no way to write three blogs in my spare time.*

*I hated to end "Ake's Pains" and I struggled to find the words to tell my faithful readers.*

*Fortunately, the newspaper cancelled the new blog after only one week before I had the chance to tell my readers I was ending "Ake's Pains". It turns out this saved me from making one of the worst decisions of my life.*

*This is one of those bizarre situations in life where you think something terrible has happened, when in reality something great just occurred; you just don't know it yet. I am so glad the newspaper dropped me or you would not be reading this right now. And if my former employer had not dumped me out on the street after 16 years of service, you would not be reading this right now. I love writing humor, so out of some bad things comes the best thing.*

*I hope you enjoyed the book. I hope it made you repeatedly laugh out loud, because that is why I do what I do. Thanks for reading.*

For the latest musings, please visit Ake's Pains blog at: http://akespains.blogspot.com

My website is: http://donake.net

Follow on twitter @theakeman

# Acknowledgements

This book only exists because of the readers of "Ake's Pains" Blog. The people who faithfully read it, the people who provide the positive feedback, the people who inspire me to raise my writing to a much higher level than I thought possible. Thank you all so much. I value you greatly.

I give much credit, respect and gratitude to my editor, Sandie Hampton. Bloggers don't have editors, but authors do. It was difficult to have my work professionally evaluated by someone after being basically freewheeling as a blogger for over four years. Sandie understands me and what I am trying to say. She was able to skillfully smooth out the rough edges to make my writing more appealing to a wider audience. I hate editors, but I love Sandie.

The illustrations are provided by Lauren Cattarin, a terrifically talented artist. I only required simple sketches, so I actually had to harness Lauren's talent a bit. She is very skilled and capable of providing so much more if required.

The cover art is by the best graphic artist in the region, Michael Gorfido. He is a great friend. His strong belief in, and enthusiasm about, this project is priceless. He won't understand what I mean by that statement because it is just Michael being Michael, and that's what makes him special.

Thanks to my good friend Lori Behrendsen for helping make some of the tough calls on editorial content. She also provided some strong emotional support for the project.

I want to thank my wife Dawn for not reading the blog. She doesn't read it because she is continuously subjected to my bizarre observations on a daily basis. And yet we are still married. If she read the blog, I'm sure it would cramp my style and nobody wants that, do they?

A big thanks to the members of the Canton (OH) Writer's Guild who took in and accepted this offbeat, weird blogger guy. They provided valuable instruction, which has improved my writing and offered much needed support and community.

And lastly, I need to thank the people whose actions prevented me from achieving what I thought I wanted, but in reality never desired. If they hadn't slammed all the doors in my face, this book would never have existed. I raise a glass and tip my hat to you all!